1735

A SPECK ON THE HORIZON

Three townships of land are granted from Boston.

Pittsfield is on the way! Only at first, it has an Indian name, Poontoosuck, which means "run for deer".

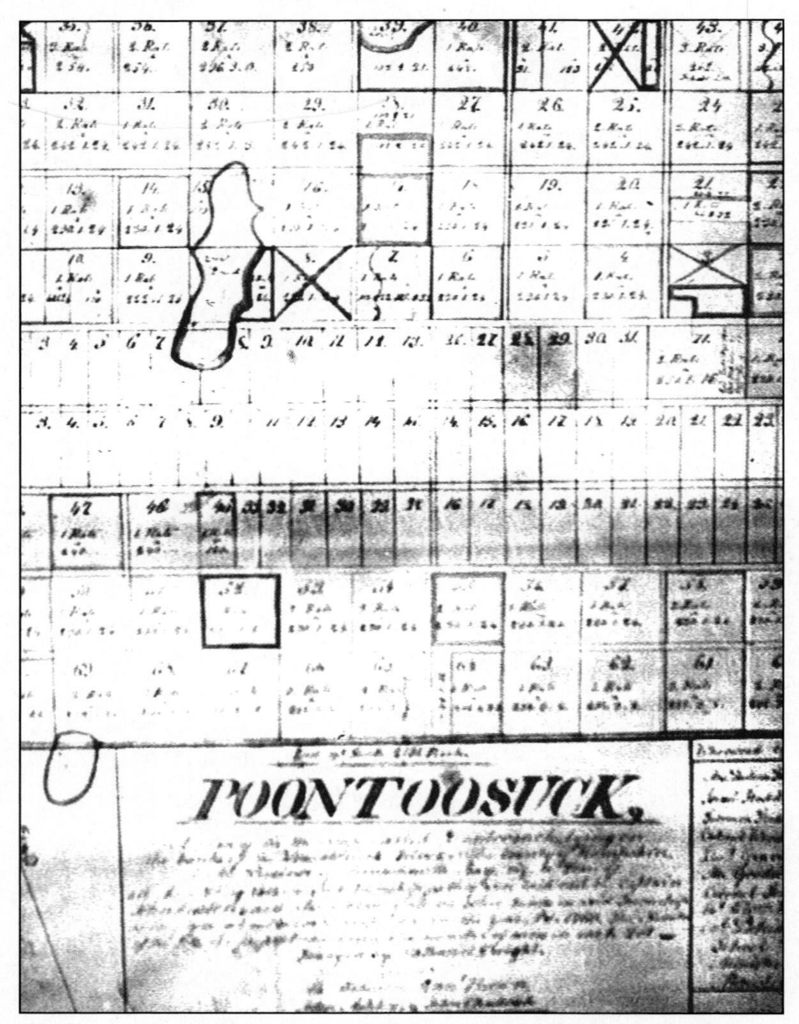

Plan of Poontoosuck *Courtesy of The Berkshire Historical Society*

The land grant lays out the details: what size the lots are to be, how many families can live in town, three lots have to be put aside for a Meeting House, a Minister's house, a school.

Before any plan can be confirmed, Colonel Jacob Wendell, who lives in Boston, steps in, buys the Poontoosuck township and ultimately arranges for a joint partnership in the property with Colonel William Stoddard. The lots go on the market immediately, but not much else happens. Then the Indians attack around the same time and really tie things up.

Col. Jacob Wendell *Courtesy of Berkshire Athenaeum*

But in 1752, an adventurous farmer, Solomon Deming from Wethersfield, Ct., starts the ball rolling. He moves his family to the East section. Charles Goodrich and others follow and in 1753, this small group is incorporated as the Proprietors of the settling lots in Poontoosuck. As they begin their new lives, they immediately turn their attention to a Meeting House: Where will it stand? How big will it be? Who will be the Minister? It is an ongoing discussion and in the middle of it all, the Indians attack again--and everything goes on hold.

olomon Deming House *Courtesy of Berkshire Athenaeum*

In 1760, however, the villagers actually agree on the size of the Meeting House and start the building. It will be another year before they can hold the first service in a building that is roughly constructed and far from finished.

Behind the scenes, other things are happening: A name change is in the works.

William Pitt is a name with meaning. This British Prime Minister is known for his resentment against the French and for encouraging the Colonists to hold their ground with the British. He is a hero throughout New England. The decision is up to the Colonial Governor, Sir Francis Bernard, who has the authority to choose a different name.

In 1761, the name changes and the town is officially incorporated as PITTSFIELD. And 1761 turns out to be a banner year because the Reverend Ebenezer Guernsey takes the pulpit in the new Meeting House, the first in a passing ministerial parade.

William Pitt *Courtesy of Berkshire Athenaeum*

Reverend Mr. Thomas Allen *Courtesy of Berkshire Athenaeum*

It takes another four years, however, before issues within the church are resolved and the Reverend Mr. Thomas Allen is ordained as the first permanent minister.

And now legends really begin…

FROM THE BEGINNING, PITTSFIELD IS A SPUNKY TOWN...

One of the first to vigorously take a stand against doing business with the British before the Revolution.

While no Revolutionary War battles are actually fought here, the women keep looms and spinning wheels busy at home making uniforms, blankets and sweaters.

In 1774, a company of Minutemen is formed under the command of Captain David Noble. Many of these men literally come from the congregation of the Meeting House, following a call to action by the Reverend Mr. Allen who delivers a sermon one Sunday--and then shows his Federalist uniform under his robes! And so the men march off to enlist. It is this same minister who wears many hats in the community--on the pulpit and as an ardent Revolutionary. A few years later, in 1777, he leads a battalion in the Battle of Bennington, Vermont as "The Fighting Parson".

Pittsfield Winter Wonderland *Photograph: Lew Mahony*

From the earliest times, Pittsfield is considered one of the most beautiful towns in all of New England. But just look at what comes naturally with the territory: towering mountain ranges, shimmering lakes and lakelets, grassy knolls, and meadows, stately forests--the fascination of changing seasons. An environment that naturally entices people to enjoy the outdoors, all year long.

Courtesy of The Berkshire Historical Society

Women rowers, c. 1880

Hiking and climbing Mt. Greylock, hunting on Old Tower Hill, fishing at Silver Lake, rowing and sailing on Lake Onota, the Berkshires largest and most beautiful body of water--families and women alone, rowing in long skirts and corsets. And when the temperature drops, there is ice fishing, sleigh ride parties, ice skating, a passion that still continues and disregards gender and age.

Most likely, it is this natural beauty that draws people to Pittsfield. There is also an intellectual stimulus attracting families with names that are familiar today: Wendell, Melville, Holmes...men who are not born here, but choose to live here. Thinking men, involved in important movements in the young country.

Most of the villagers are well-to-do farmers with sound New England values and education. Comfortable, but not especially fashionable. They drive fine horses and travel to services on horseback, wagons, even on foot. After the benediction they leave promptly for Sunday dinner and chores which have to be finished by sundown. And everyone--lawyers, teachers, ministers--has a farm. For the most part, they are not "Gentlemen Farmers". These people get into the earth and farm as their families have for years.

Oliver Wendell Holmes *Courtesy of Berkshire Athenaeum*

What about the day to day? The men raise barns and houses, while women quilt, spin and work inside. Quilting bees can be very competitive and frequently teams are formed: Singles against Marrieds. Sisters against Friends. Often, as the young women work, Paradise Lost, Virgil and other classics are read out loud. And they learn to play the forte piano or another instrument to enhance their charms.

Music brings people together and Pittsfield is very social.

Everyone dances and goes to concerts. They all play games. Board games like Nine Men's Morris, and cards, especially Poker, when allowed, and ball. Lots of ball. And with large volunteer fire companies and slews of town meetings, it's easy to make friends.

Food through the centuries, is always a good reason to get together. Today we invite friends for cocktails or a pot-luck supper. In 18th century Pittsfield, you go to a "kettle-drum" (an elaborate afternoon tea with scones, jam, and cakes), a "small and early" (a hearty cold supper with sliced turkey or ham) a lavish "5 o'clock dinner" (with fresh fish, a roast, vegetables, and pudding). And who would want to miss the fun of a taffy pull or an oyster roast in the kitchen on a cold night?

And so, in 1783, the Revolutionary War is officially over. The Treaty of Paris is signed. Celebration is the mood of the countryside. The whole town joins in a victory party at John Chandler Williams house, later known as The Peace Party House. What marks an occasion better than a parade! But in Pittsfield, not any parade, the first 4th of July Parade! And a legend takes off on North Street.

The Peace Party House *Courtesy of The Berkshire Historical Societ*

Overall, a way of life is set in the 18th century: indoors/outdoors

1791
A LEGEND IS TAKING SHAPE

The villagers are settling in.

The current buzz has a familiar ring: A Meeting House. A new one!

The first one, built 30 years ago, is falling apart. The walls, the floors, everything on the inside always needs repair. The outside is even worse. Windows are always broken with glass always scattered about the grounds. How these windows get broken is kind of its own legend. And key to the new Meeting House, which will be in a class of its own. The pride of this New England community. And sort of a toy to the parishioners.

What will this Meeting House be like? A towering structure with the grandeur of the US Capitol and Faneuil Hall in Boston, and designed by the same architect, Charles Bulfinch. The parishioners have agreed on the size, but now the major controversy is Where! Location, location, location, even in 1791. Everyone is determined it must be seen by passing travelers as well as locals and visitors. Finally they vote on a site and reach a consensus.

There is only one problem: a beautiful old elm tree that's hundreds of years old has to be cut down.

Park Square and the old elm tree, c. 1830 *Courtesy of The Berkshire Historical Society*

The day comes and the whole town is watching as the ax starts to make its mark. On the third chop, a young woman who loves this elm tree, Lucretia Williams, throws herself in front of the tree. Everyone gasps.

And then, John Chandler Williams, now Lucretia's husband, steps on to the green and offers a compromise: he will give a part of his extensive property to the town for the Meeting House. By moving the building a few feet, it gets even greater visibility—and the elm tree is saved.

And so, the villagers move forward. They select the finest woods from neighboring forests, choose artisans to do the work and take an active interest in the elegant interior. All very exciting but that is just the beginning. Another vote and another decision: Build a Town Hall--and actually cut down the wear and tear on the inside of the building. The plan is to have two floors. On the first level, two rooms will house two schools where generations of Pittsfield kids will study. Upstairs is a mix of town business and culture. Tables and chairs are arranged for the Council, Selectmen and Town Clerk. There are also rows of seats for concerts, lectures and social gatherings. So, the Town Hall absorbs most of the action and the inside of the beautiful Meeting House is safe.

The towering elm tree 1856 *Courtesy of Berkshire Athenaeum*

Ultimately this Meeting House will put the spotlight on everyday life in the 18th century and what people do when they aren't attending services or meetings or working. It will go on to make sports history by proving that baseball was born right here in Pittsfield and--boys will always be boys.

Remember the broken glass around the building? Well, the parishioners finally figure out the cause. They call on a Selectman, Woodbridge Little, who is also a lawyer. He drafts a bylaw which the Council passes. A simple statement which makes Pittsfield a legend in sports history.

"...for the preservation of the windows in the new Meeting House...no Person or Inhabitant of said town, shall be permitted to play at any game Called Base ball, Bat ball, Cat, Fives or any other Game or Games with Balls, within the Distance of Eighty Yards from said Meeting House."

Passed by the Pittsfield Council in 1791

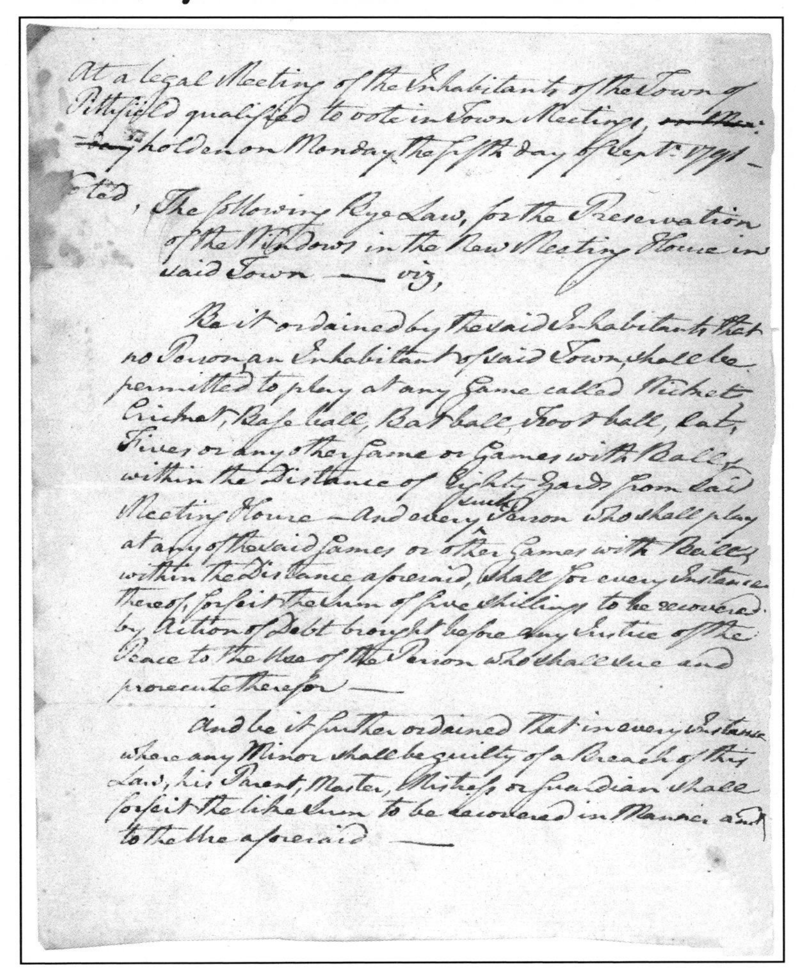

At a legal Meeting of the Inhabitants of the Town of Pittsfield qualified to vote in Town Meetings, holden on Monday the fifth day of Sept. 1791 –

Voted, The following Bye Law, for the Preservation of the Windows in the New Meeting House in said Town — viz,

Be it ordained by the said Inhabitants that no Person an Inhabitant of said Town, shall be permitted to play at any Game called Wicket, Cricket, Baseball, Batball, Football, Cats, Fives or any other Game or Games with Balls within the Distance of Eighty Yards from said Meeting House – And every such Person who shall play at any of the said Games or other Games with Balls within the Distance aforesaid, shall for every Instance thereof, forfeit the Sum of five shillings to be recovered by Action of Debt brought before any Justice of the Peace to the Use of the Person who shall sue and prosecute therefor —

And be it further ordained that in every Instance where any Minor shall be guilty of a Breach of this Law, his Parent, Master, Mistress or Guardian shall forfeit the like Sum to be recovered in Manner and to the Use aforesaid —

Courtesy of Berkshire Athenaeum

It is this Pittsfield by-law, which clearly establishes the earliest mention of baseball in the United States, is made right here in Pittsfield, Massachusetts.

The original document is at home in Pittsfield. A copy hangs in the Baseball Hall of Fame in Cooperstown, New York.

Even with the by-law, the Common continues to be the favorite spot for playing ball. When it gets out of hand, you can be sure John Chandler Williams appears on the green, and the game comes to a speedy ending.

PITTSFIELD ON A ROLL... KIND OF

Improvement is clearly the focus of the village.

In 1792, the Council votes to use the land around the Meeting House for a town burial ground rather than an open green. A neat white fence will protect the "residents". The council votes to allow Dr. Timothy Childs to build a medicine store nearby. This land has a fence too, which connects with the cemetery fence.

And this marks the beginning of Park Square.

A few years after Lucretia Williams saves the elm tree, she takes the stage again. The Williams have many buttonwood trees on their property. They are trendy shade trees, but John and Lucretia prefer elms. However, the world being what it is, they don't move quickly. Then John goes off on a business trip and Lucretia has all the buttonwoods cut down. John's work is cut out for him when he returns. Together this enterprising couple does something thoughtful again. They carefully research and choose Dutch elms, and so, because of Lucretia and John Williams, a colonnade of these special elm trees is planted around Park Square.

By S. Barnes

The Bulfinch Church and the Old Elm Tree *Courtesy of Berkshire Athenaeum*

A little aside about the headstrong Lucretia: She is the daughter of Colonel Israel Williams, an active Tory. As the mood of the country changes, he is put in jail. Lucretia, then seventeen, brings food to him in jail every day. In 1786 she marries John Chandler Williams, an ardent supporter of American independence. Their gracious home is the scene of many political gatherings but the outspoken Lucretia remains a Tory and always refers to the American Revolution as the "Rebellion".

The Williams family continues to be an ongoing presence in Pittsfield. In 1815 a young lawyer, Edward Newton, marries their middle daughter, Sarah. A relative newcomer to Pittsfield, Newton is quickly accepted into the town's inner circles. Ultimately he continues his in-law's philanthropy by planting more elm trees around Park Square and laying out roads around the common. Sidewalks soon follow. As the town evolves, you will find The Hon. Edward Newton's name listed in many major ventures. It is in his plot in Pittsfield Cemetery where Lucretia and John Chandler Williams are buried.

Park Square 1865: looking south at Bank Row — *Courtesy of Berkshire Athenaeum*

If you drive along Wahconah Street, watch for the cemetery gates. Pittsfield Cemetery is one of a few in the United States designed as a park, giving visitors a beautiful environment for reflection.

Spend a little time in these tree lined grounds and remember the dedication of John and Lucretia Williams. You'll find many of the other legendary families in town resting here, too.

The Gates to the Pittsfield Cemetery donated by the Thomas Allen family in 1885 *Courtesy of Berkshire Athenaeum*

St. John's Lake, a quiet spot in the cemetery *Courtesy of Berkshire Athenaeum*

1800 - 1859

1800
- Phinehas Allen moves to Pittsfield and starts The Pittsfield Sun
- Arthur Scholfield comes to Pittsfield with his wool carding machine
- James Colt builds legendary house
- The American Hotel changes name to William Clark Hotel. The Landlord, Captain Joseph Merrick, is a staunch Republican, who refuses to serve Federalists

1801
- Zenas Crane builds a paper mill on the Housatonic

1806
- Miss Nancy Hinsdale school opens. Later becomes Miss Hall's School

1807
- Elkanah Watson starts Berkshire Agricultural Society

1808
- Rev. Mr. Allen sells his original lots to Federalists, who open Pittsfield House on Park Square

1810
- Berkshire Bank, Pittsfield's first bank, opens on Park Square
- Elkanah Watson organizes the First Agricultural Fair in U.S. on Park Square

1812
- Lemuel Pomeroy buys Scholfield's textile business and starts Pittsfield Woolen and Cotton factory
- Campbell's Coffee House opens on Bank Row. Sort of a "resort" for British officers. Today: Patrick's Pub

1815
- Edward Newton marries Sarah Williams. He continues family philanthropy of John and Lucretia Williams

1818
- Berkshire Agricultural Bank opens

1823
- Berkshire Medical Institution, first Med School in Western Massachusetts opens on Park Square

1825
- Pontoosuc Woolen Mill chartered
- Thaddeus Clapp hired as Superintendent

1826
- Rev. Chester Dewey opens European-style Gymnasium school for boys

1832
- A new Town Hall is built on North side of Park Square. Lemuel Pomeroy pays for it
- St. Stephen's church, the First Episcopal Church in Pittsfield, built by Edward Newton

1835
- Berkshire Mutual Fire Insurance Company organized
- Nathan Willis is President

1840
- Pittsfield population about 4,000
- Pittsfield Baseball Club opens

1846
- Berkshire County Savings Bank opens on Park Square
- Blacks form Second Congregational Church and dedicate Meeting House on Onota Street
- Exchange Hotel opens on site of James Colt house

1849
- Dr. Oliver Wendell Holmes builds Holmesdale on Canoe Meadows, Great-Grandson of Jacob Wendell

1850
- Population of Pittsfield about 7000
- Pittsfield Library Association formed with 800 books
- Herman Melville comes to live at Arrowhead until 1863. He writes Moby Dick here
- West's Block opens
- Pittsfield Cemetery dedicated

1851
- George Nixon Briggs, former Massachusetts Governor, starts Berkshire Life Insurance Company on Park Square
- Western Massachusetts Mutual Fire Insurance Company starts

1853
- Pittsfield Coal Gas Company starts and gas brightens the town
- First President is Thomas F. Plunkett

1857
- Moses England opens his first store on North Street

1859
- First Intercollegiate Baseball Game between Williams/Amherst, played at Pittsfield Baseball Club: Baseball and Chess/Muscle and Mind
- Amherst wins

THEN, ABOUT 10 YEARS AFTER THE MEETING HOUSE IS FINISHED, PITTSFIELD BEGINS TO MAKE NEWS...

New people...New businesses.

It is 1800, and at the suggestion of his famous uncle, the Reverend Mr. Thomas Allen, Phinehas Allen moves to Pittsfield, and starts to publish The Pittsfield Sun.

Phinehas is 24 and has worked as a journeyman on a newspaper in Springfield. He publishes The Pittsfield Sun every Tuesday in a plant opposite the Meeting House. Readers find local, international, social and political news items along with chatty bits of homily. Famous names become personalities. The world seems closer.

Phinehas Allen *Courtesy of Berkshire Athenaeum*

That same year, 1800, Arthur Scholfield, a Scotsman from Leeds, who smuggled his wool-carding machine out of England, comes to Pittsfield and takes the town in a profitable new direction.

Scholfield revolutionizes cloth making—and the town is never the same again. Not only quality, but quantity changes. It is here in Pittsfield where cloth for the inaugural suit of President James Madison is woven.

Soon the villagers are raising large flocks of Merino sheep, pastures start to replace forests, sheep shearing becomes big business and an exciting new competition for kids and adults. The challenge: how much, how quickly and how creatively each one can shear wool.

In 1812, one of the town's leading figures, Lemuel Pomeroy, buys Scholfield's business and starts The Pittsfield Woolen and Cotton Factory. It flourishes until 1893.

Shortly after Pomeroy buys Scholfield's mill, he hires Thaddeus Clapp, who has a remarkable instinct for the business. A perfectionist, Clapp soon becomes skilled in all phases of manufacturing wool fabric and competent enough to run the factory.

Lemuel Pomeroy *Courtesy of Berkshire Athenaeum*

In 1825, when the Pontoosuc (spelling changes) Woolen Company is chartered,Clapp is hired as Superintendent. Thaddeus Clapp marries Elizabeth Colt and their eldest son, also Thaddeus, continues the Clapp legacy in textile manufacturing. The Pontoosuc mills keep running into the 1920's. Son Thaddeus marries Lucy Goodrich from another old Pittsfield family and becomes an active presence in politics and education. You can walk past his gracious home on Wendell Avenue, an enduring sign of an early successful industrialist.

Thaddeus Clapp *Courtesy of Berkshire Athenaeum*

Today the Thaddeus Clapp House is a very special B&B.

Pittsfield's agrarian economy keeps on growing.

Elkanah Watson *Courtesy of Berkshire Athenaeum*

Following this trend, Elkanah Watson, an innovative gentleman farmer, buys Henry Van Schaack's beautiful mansion and extensive property. He has plans to start a model farm to test new plantings and techniques. Watson goes on to organize The Berkshire Agricultural Society, providing a unique platform for farmers and farming. Its membership comes from many states and builds quickly.

A few years later, Watson organizes the first Agricultural Fair in America. Naturally Merino sheep are the main exhibit. The Fair takes place, would you believe, under Lucretia's elm tree and attracts working farmers and women, as well as "Gentlemen Farmers".

Some fifty years later Lucretia's elm tree becomes diseased and finally has to be cut down. Guess what: the three chops the ax made all those years ago are still visible! The tree is now 340 years old and 128 feet tall! When you are on Park Square, look for the plaque commemorating the Agricultural Fair in 1810 and Lucretia's famous tree, now called The Pittsfield Elm: 1524-1864.

Lucretia's Elm Tree *Courtesy of The Berkshire Historical Society*

SITE OF THE
FIRST AGRICULTURAL FAIR
IN AMERICA
1810
AND
THE PITTSFIELD ELM
1524 - 1864

The Plaque on Park Square

Photograph: Phyllis Kerle

CATTLE-SHOW

AND FAIR

OF THE

Berkshire County Agricultural Society,

AT PITTSFIELD,

Wednesday, Thursday and Friday, October 7th, 8th & 9th

The 47th Anniversary of the Berkshire Agricultural Society, will be held on the 7th, 8th and 9th days of October next, at the new Cattle Show Grounds in Pittsfield, which are prepared for the purpose.

All the Exhibitions and all the Exercises of the three days will be on said grounds, and in the building thereon.

The exhibition of all kinds of animals for premiums, (except horses,) and of all manufactured articles and implements of machinery, will be on the First Day.

The exhibition of Horses for premiums, as well as for show and trial of speed, will be on the Second Day.

The Plowing Match, the Annual Address, the Reports of Committees, and the Delivery of Premiums, will be on the Third Day.

The Cattle Show Grounds, owned by the Society, are enclosed, and are by law under the control of the Officers of the Society, and no persons can enter upon the same except according to the regulations prescribed by the Society.

CAUTION.

EVERY PERSON GETTING INTO THE ENCLOSURE IN VIOLATION OF THE RULES OF THE SOCIETY, IS LIABLE BY THE REVISED STATUTES TO A FINE OF *FIVE DOLLARS* AND WILL BE IMMEDIATELY PROSECUTED THEREFOR.

IMPROVEMENTS.

The Entrance to the Grounds, and the roads on the same, and the Horse Track and the Buildings have been greatly improved the present year.

PASTURAGE.

Cattle intended for Premium, will be admitted to the Grounds on Tuesday, where they will have good pasture without charge.

FRUIT.

Large glass cases for the proper exhibition and protection of Fruit, have been placed in the Hall.

ARTICLES FOR EXHIBITION.

All Articles for Exhibition in the Hall must be removed at the close of the Exhibition.

THE GROUNDS.

All persons, except those in charge of property, will be required to leave the grounds at 7 o'clock on the evening of each day.

CHOPPING OR LOGGING MATCH.

At four o'clock, P. M., of Wednesday, there will be a Chopping Match on the grounds under the superintendence of a Committee. Regulations made known at the time. Four premiums, $4, $3, $2, $1.

SPADING MATCH.

At 4 o'clock P. M., of Thursday there will be a Spading Match on the grounds. Four Premiums, $4, $3, $2, $1.

FOOT RACING.

There will be opportunity for Foot Racing under the patronage of private gentlemen, when the track is not occupied by the Society.

AWARD OF PREMIUMS AND VIOLATION OF RULES.

If it should appear that any competitor for a premium has made use of any dishonorable measures, by which the objects of the Society have been defeated, or the rules and regulations violated, such person shall not only be rendered incapable of being ever after a competitor for any premium of the Society, but may be proceeded against according to By-laws.

The reports of the several Committees of the Society, shall be submitted after the annual Cattle Show and Fair, to the Executive Committee, for Examination, and if said Committee find that any premiums have been awarded by mistake or in violation of the rules, and regulations of the Society, said Committee shall require the person or persons, so receiving the premiums to return the same; and shall recommend any proceedings in such case or cases, as to them may seem proper.

Said meeting of the executive committee shall be held on the last Monday of October next, at two o'clock, P. M., at the Berkshire Hotel in Pittsfield.

All articles for premium, in the Hall, must remain in the same until 3 o'clock of the second day. Although all animals, except horses, and all articles for premium, must be entered and examined by the Committees on the First Day, they may be exhibited on the other days, the room and accommodations being ample; and it is desired these exhibitions may be continued, in order to give full opportunities for the Committees to make repeated examinations and to give the public full opportunity to view the same.

Grounds are set apart to be occupied by Victuallers, Pedlars, &c., and are under the charge of Mr. John Spencer.

ARRANGEMENTS.

FIRST DAY.

The Treasurer will attend at his office at the entrance to the grounds, to receive dues from Members, to issue Certificates of Life Membership, to receive Fees from those going upon the grounds, and to furnish Tickets of Admission to members. Persons wishing to become Members will apply to him.

All animals, except Horses, proposed for premium, must be entered with the Secretary at the large building, by eleven o'clock, A. M., of the first day.

All articles of manufacture, Butter, Cheese, Agricultural and Horticultural Productions, Fruits, Flowers, Agricultural Implements, Specimens, Models, must be delivered to Mr. James H. Butler, in the Hall.

The Stock will be arranged in distinct divisions and pens, under the direction of persons appointed to take charge of this part of the Show.

The Horse Course will be open the first day for the exercise of Horses. All horses for premium must be entered by 9 o'clock, A. M., of the second day.

SECOND DAY.

9 o'clock, A. M.—Grand Cavalcade of all Horses entered for premium, around the course.

10 o'clock.—Exhibition of Mares and Colts before the Committee.

11 o'clock,—Exhibition of Carriage Horses.

12 o'clock, M.—Exhibition of Draft Horses.

1 o'clock,—Exhibition of Single Horses.

2 o'clock,—Exhibition of Stud Horses.

3 o'clock,—Exhibition of Young Horses.

4 o'clock,—Exhibition of Trotting Horses.

THIRD DAY.

The Plowing Match will commence on the enclosed grounds, at 9 o'clock, A. M. Entries must be made by 4 o'clock, P. M. of the second day.

11 o'clock.—The Society will assemble in the Exhibition Hall to attend the public exercises, hear reports, &c., when the competitors for premiums are requested to attend.

ORDER OF EXERCISES IN THE HALL.

1. Music.
2. Prayer by Rev. Mr. Alden of Lenox.
3. Music.
4. Address by the President, E. Williams, Esq., of Richmond.
5. Music.
6. Reports of Awarding Committees.

The following persons constitute the Committees of Awards, viz:—

AGRICULTURE.

Summer and Fall Crops.—Charles K. Tracy, Edward S. Rowley, Benj. Hall.

CHEESE.

Reuben Wood, Robert E. Galpin, R. Columbus Brown.

BUTTER AND BREAD.

Harmon L. Bates, Benjamin Baldwin, J. L. Northrop.

VEGETABLES, SEED, &c.

James H. Butler, Simeon M. Dean, William H. Nichols, Alberto Richards, John S. Jordan, Lorenzo H. Merriam.

FRUITS.

James D. Adams, Benjamin F. Mills, Samuel G. Goodrich, Geo. Harmon, Geo. W. Kaffin, E. W. B. Canning, Harvey Cole.

FLORAL DEPARTMENT.

Edward Pomeroy, Mrs. E. Williams, Mrs. John F. Arnold, Mrs. C. T. Fenn, Mrs. D. J. Dodge.

HOUSEHOLD MANUFACTURES.

First Division.—Edwin F. Jenks, J. H. Mills, Elmer Smith, John H. Strong, Wm. W. Carson.

Second Division.—Henry Chickering, Abel Kittredge, E. Marshall Crane, John F. Arnold, William Hadsell.

AGRICULTURAL AND MECHANICAL IMPLEMENTS.

Lyman Fenn, Solomon L. Russel, P. S. Palmer, William W. Goodman, Asahel Sherman.

DOMESTIC ANIMALS—FIRST DIVISION.

Fat Cattle.—Henry A. Barton, John B. Wells, John Sherrill, 2d, Pliny M. Shaylor, Leonard Tuttle.

SECOND DIVISION.

Working Oxen.—Josiah S. Wilson, H. D. Palmer, Edward Cheeseman, Edward S. Rowley, Eli R. Deming.

THIRD DIVISION.

Three and Two Years Old.—Franklin B. Cone, William Harrison, Henry B. Brewster, Albert G. Belden, Joseph Foot.

FOURTH DIVISION.

Milch Cows.—Phinehas M. Wright, Samuel M. Cooper, Elias Wright, Wm. E. Johnson, Henry Noble.

FIFTH DIVISION.

Breeding Cows.—Henry Smith, Aaron P. Bagg, Franklin Gaston, David Smith, E. C. Bridges.

SIXTH DIVISION.

Two Year Old Heifers.—John E. Merrill, Amos B. Thatcher, Daniel D. Kendall, John Gordon, Martin L. Ingalls.

SEVENTH DIVISION.

Bulls.—Henry Dresser, Levi Beach, Nathaniel Cook, James Foot, Chapin Converse.

EIGHTH DIVISION.

Fine Wool Sheep.—Seymour Wilcox, Henry Putnam, Theodore J. Williams, Walter Richards, Alanson Jones.

NINTH DIVISION.

Coarse Wool Sheep.—Elijah N. Hubbard, Henry Warden, jr., Franklin Farnham, Ira A. Smith, Nathaniel Hague.

TENTH DIVISION.

Swine.—Phinehas Harmon, William McMurray, Reed Mills, Crocker Thatcher, Mark Laird.

ELEVENTH DIVISION.

Poultry.—Samuel M. Bowerman, Wm. P. Churchill, John Branning, Thos. Cole, Charles R. Dean.

TWELFTH DIVISION.

Matched Horses.—Amasa Rice, James Dewell, Charles S. Thatcher, T. Sabin, George Sabin.

THIRTEENTH DIVISION.

Single Horses and Stallions.—Socrates Squier, Ira A. Smith, James E. Hall, A. B. Howland, Samuel Fisher.

FOURTEENTH DIVISION.

Trotting Horses.—Robert Pomeroy, Franklin B. Cone, Cyrus Crosby, William Pollock, John M. Cole, Seymour Crane, Porter E. Gowdy, Luke Miller, William C. Allen, Stephen E. Gay.

FIFTEENTH DIVISION.

Breeding Mares and Colts.—Edson Sexton, A. C. Butler, Frances Deming, Horatio N. Little, Orrin Benedict, Nelson Joyner.

SIXTEENTH DIVISION.

Young Horses.—Charles B. Nye, Jas. Waterman, Alonzo Gamon, Marshall Butler, Chester Holt, Ezra Sherman.

PLOWING MATCH.

Committee.—Joshua R. Lawton, A. P. Merrill, Solomon L. Russell, Orrin Curtis, Otis Peck, Eli Bradley, George O. Peck, Asahel Foote, Justus Tower, Jonathan Condee, Timothy Case.

MARSHALS.

The following gentlemen are appointed Marshals of the day:—

MAJ. HENRY S. BRIGGS, *Chief Marshal.*

Assistants.

E. J. Nichols, Amasa Rice,
E. G. Brown, Geo. O. Peck,
Franklin B. Cone, Robert Pomeroy,
Edward Learned, S. & A. Churchill,
John E. Merrill, E. W. [illegible],
Edward B. Fowler, John M. Cole,
Samuel I. Pollard, Franklin B. Gates.

FEES FOR ENTERING THE GROUNDS.

10 cents for entering the Grounds and to all the Exhibitions.
30 cents a Season Ticket, as a ticket for the three days.
13 cents for a single carriage.
50 cents for a season ticket for a single carriage.
$1 for a season ticket for a double carriage.
50 cents per day for use of stables on the Grounds.

Persons not members, must pay to the Treasurer the sum of two dollars for the privilege of entering for any premium of the society, except those on Household Manufactures.

Any person by subscribing to the By-Laws, and paying one dollar annually, can become a member of the society.

Life Memberships, for males $10, and for females $5.

Persons not Members may obtain tickets at the entrance, or at the Agricultural Store, or Dodge & Hubbard's in the village.

Tickets of free admission will be furnished to members, for themselves and teams, but not for other passengers.

Pedlars, Victuallers, Auctioneers, &c., will be required to keep upon the grounds assigned them.

The Marshals are clothed by law with power to preserve and enforce order, and will take care that all regulations of the society be enforced.

COMMITTEE OF ARRANGEMENTS.

Robert Colt, J. Henry Rowley,
Geo. S. Willis, E. H. Kellogg,
D. D. Kendall, Henry Colt,
Wm. W. Goodman, Simeon M. Dean,
Henry M. Peirson, Wm. H. Nichols.

Reed, Hull & Peirson, Job Printers, Francis' Block.

broadside, for the Berkshire Cattle Show *Courtesy of The Berkshire Historical Society*

As business grows in the 19th century, another local landmark company gets started. In 1801, Zenas Crane builds a paper mill on the banks of the Housatonic. It will ultimately become the oldest mill in continuous use in the United States.

Zenas Crane's father, Stephen, has already made his niche in paper. During the 18th century he produces a special type of currency paper that Paul Revere buys and prints to help finance the American Revolution. Revere, the famous horseman, is also a fine silversmith.

Zenas Crane, at 24 years *Courtesy of Crane & Co. Archives*

From the onset, Zenas Crane has a commitment to a standard of quality which he builds into Crane & Company. Fine quality paper needs cotton rags which are not plentiful. As the industry grows and becomes more competitive, many companies switch to wood pulp which produces a cheaper product. Zenas frequently runs ads asking women to sell him their old rags. Although rags are hard to get, he refuses to lower his standards. Then Phinehas Allen, publisher of The Pittsfield Sun and a close friend, makes a point in a creative way: he prints special editions of the newspaper on Crane's quality paper. Today these 19th century clippings are still clear and easy to read. A testimonial to these men and their ongoing quest for the best.

Zenas Crane Jr., grandson of Zenas *Courtesy of Crane & Co. Archives*

When Zenas retires in 1842, his sons Zenas Marshall and James Brewer take over the company. Under their guidance Crane creates a technique that stops a form of counterfeiting and in 1879, Murray Crane (Zenas Marshall's son) wins the bid for the company to produce U.S. bank note paper in their handsome building, known as The Government Mill. It is the oldest contract in effect with the United States Government. Today, Crane supplies paper for many foreign currencies and recently bought facilities in Europe to supply paper for the Euro--a company always moving with the times. And Crane started making fine stationery after the Civil War!

In the 21st century, the little company Zenas started over 200 years ago, is the classiest stationery and art paper producer in the United States, sought after around the world.

The Crane signature is everywhere in Pittsfield. It is Zenas Crane Jr. we can thank for the fascinating Berkshire Museum of Art and Natural History. Four generations later, the family name is a constant in the city's major cultural and art ventures.

The Government Mill. Owned and managed by Crane & Co — *Courtesy of Berkshire Athenaeum*

AN EARLY PART OF THE PITTSFIELD SCENE: PEOPLE OF COLOR

From the beginning a liberal city.

Many blacks are newly freed slaves. Many are slaves working alongside the farmers. It is the black's knowledge of farming and crops that helps to develop a strong agrarian economy which supports rural areas as well as the growing town.

Some slavery persists here until 1783, in spite of the Pittsfield Bill of Rights, written in 1779, which clearly states "no man can be deprived of liberty".

Overall, Pittsfield has little segregation and a fairly liberal attitude toward blacks. By 1800, more than 5% of the city is black, a high percentage compared with other cities. Many blacks are successful entrepreneurs. The first may be John Persip.

Alfred Persip *Courtesy of The Berkshire Eagle*

This stow-away from Portugal, turns out to be a creative and enterprising gardener who starts a landscaping business in 1790. Persip marries soon after and begins a family which is still a presence in Pittsfield. John's son marries Alice Hamilton, another early black family whose descendents are still in town.

A few generations later, Alfred, his great-grandson, continues the legacy of landscaping into the 20th century until 1984, when he dies. Alfred's daughter, Eleanor is a highly regarded teacher in Pittsfield's school system and a noted golfer. Ellie's Uncle John, and Alfred's brother, is a popular caterer who lives here in Pittsfield until his death at 96 in 1983.

The Persips c. 1890 *Courtesy of Eleanor Persip*

The Persips and Hamiltons, like many blacks in the 19th Century, are active in the military and both families serve in the famous 54th Black Regiment during the Civil War.

Alfred Persip is the first black in Pittsfield to enlist in WW I. His brother Charles soon follows. It is Charles who becomes a charter member of American Legion Post 68 on Wendell Avenue and in 1983, it is named after him on Persip Day. Near the new Transportation Center on a corner of North Street and Columbus Avenue is Persip Park with a mural showing the Persip Brothers in uniform and honoring them for their involvement with the troops in WW I I.

Grandmother Persip with 6 of her 11 sons c. 1915 Courtesy of Eleanor Persip

Charles Persip Courtesy of The Berkshire Historical Societ

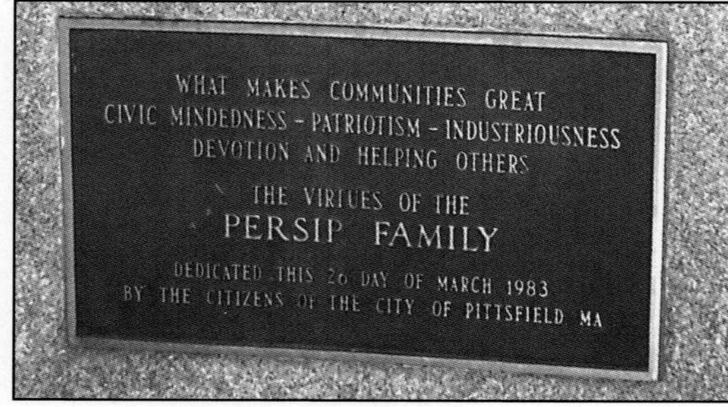

The tribute in Persip Park Photograph: Phyllis Kerle

An even more remarkable tribute is a plaque dedicated to the family for their commitment to the city. Look for it and salute the legendary Persips, still in the homestead on Pomeroy Avenue, and very much part of today's Pittsfield scene.

Ironically, some segregation is evident in Lucretia and John Chandler Williams' Meeting House, the First Congregational Church, even though it has an active group of black parishioners. At some point, the blacks decide to build their own church.

In 1846, the Second Congregational Church is dedicated. Today, 159 years later, it is one of Pittsfield's most popular and active churches with gospel music that attracts people from many places. In all these years the church has only had three ministers.

It is from this pulpit in 1850, four years after the church opens its doors, that Samuel Harrison gets his start as a minister. A black man destined to be one of Pittsfield's treasures.

A voice for people who are voiceless, the Reverend Samuel Harrison. Born in Philadelphia in 1818, he is trained by his uncle to be a shoemaker. This skill helps to pay for his education. An excellent and dedicated student whose heart is set on the ministry, Harrison develops a forceful style of speaking which leads him to the Pittsfield church. But he cannot ignore the issue of slavery during this war period.

The Reverend Samuel Harrison Courtesy of Berkshire Athenaeum

In 1862, Harrison resigns to work with Frederick Douglass, the abolitionist and founder of the National Freedman's Relief Society. Soon after, he is named Chaplain of the 54th Massachusetts Regiment, most of whom are black soldiers from Pittsfield. In the midst of the war Harrison is a fierce advocate for black equality and recognition.

The struggle affects him physically and emotionally and he is Honorably Discharged for medical reasons. Discouraged and in poor health, he has little money because his paychecks are delayed as happens to many black soldiers.

Courtesy of Berkshire Athenaeum

The Second Congregational Church

Harrison moves to Rhode Island for a few years and then, in 1872, returns to Pittsfield and the Second Congregational Church. He uses the pulpit to champion the cause of African-American equality and racial integration.

Reverend Harrison's home on Third Street, is being restored as a tribute to this remarkable man. Drive by and you will see it has a ways to go before visitors can walk through--but it is easy to imagine his family of 13 children living there. Ellen, his wife, dies in the 1880's, but Reverend Harrison continues to spread his message until 1900, when he dies at the age of 82.

Harrison's legacy as Minister, Chaplain, advocate, activist, father is legendary... another Pittsfield man of vision.

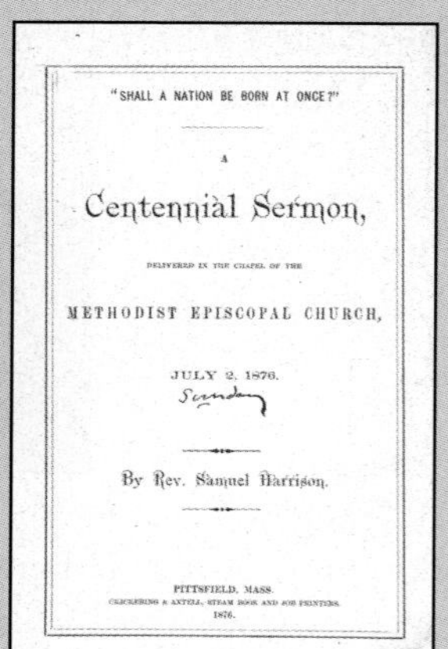
"SHALL A NATION BE BORN AT ONCE?"

A

Centennial Sermon,

DELIVERED IN THE CHAPEL OF THE

METHODIST EPISCOPAL CHURCH,

JULY 2, 1876.

Sunday

By Rev. Samuel Harrison.

PITTSFIELD, MASS.

CHICKERING & AXTELL, STEAM BOOK AND JOB PRINTERS.

1876.

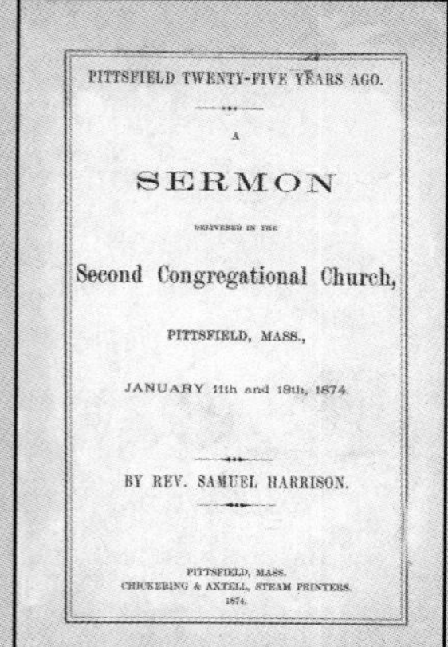
PITTSFIELD TWENTY-FIVE YEARS AGO.

A

SERMON

DELIVERED IN THE

Second Congregational Church,

PITTSFIELD, MASS.,

JANUARY 11th and 18th, 1874.

BY REV. SAMUEL HARRISON.

PITTSFIELD, MASS.

CHICKERING & AXTELL, STEAM PRINTERS.

1874.

The sermons of Reverend Samuel Harrison
Courtesy of Berkshire Athenaeum

THE TEXTURE AND THE SKYLINE OF PITTSFIELD KEEPS CHANGING...

And Park Square is always at the center of the action.

In 1823, the Berkshire Medical Institution, the first medical school in Western Massachusetts opens. It is the most prestigious school in town.

Berkshire Medical Institution — *Courtesy of The Berkshire Historical Society*

Schools are springing up all around Pittsfield. In 1826, Lemuel Pomeroy, of textile fame, buys land for a high school. The Reverend Chester Dewey uses that property to open a boy's school based on the European Gymnasium for studying ancient and modern languages, moral and religious teachings. Mr. Dillingham's private boarding school for boys is already in town, as are several schools for girls, with a curriculum more suitable for young ladies. Today Miss Hall's School on Holmes Road follows a tradition of special study for young women.

Education has a history in Pittsfield.

Pomeroy's Town Hall *Courtesy of The Berkshire Historical Society*

And so does Park Square. Around 1830, the son-in-law of John and Lucretia Williams, (remember Edward Newton?) well... Newton has become an Episcopalian, and wants to build the first Episcopal Church in Pittsfield.

Newton chooses the North side of the Square. A complicated move because Dewey's school is there. Tempers flare. But Newton is reasonable and decides to use part of his property for the church. Only that location borders Lemuel Pomeroy's land. More trouble. However, Pomeroy comes up with a great idea: Move the school a few blocks away and use that site for a new Town Hall which the village needs and which he will pay for!

Pomeroy then makes an arrangement with the Council for Newton to build his church on the opposite corner. Hop Scotch. That's the deal and everyone's happy.

Today Pomeroy's Town Hall, built in 1832, and Newton's Episcopal Church, St. Stephen's, sit staunchly on their respective corners. A sidelight: the first funeral at St. Stephen's is for John Chandler Williams, Newton's Father-in-law.

St. Stephen's Episcopal Church, 1832 *Courtesy of The Berkshire Historical Society*

By 1850, Pittsfield's population has grown to 7000. There is a paper mill, a quarry, factories for hats, brooms, tinware, silverware, textiles--the town is on the move. And the villagers are thinking about a city form of government, a major step which takes forty years to complete.

As business grows, the need for various services grows too. Prestigious Park Square is the kick-off point. In 1846, next to the Medical School on the South side of the Square, the Berkshire County Savings Bank opens its doors in a small wooden building. The first account for $25, is opened by David Stockbridge, a Pittsfield laborer.

But even in the 19th century, banks move around. Within a few years Berkshire County Savings crosses the Square and rents space in City Hall, the one Pomeroy built in 1832. The Pittsfield National Bank and the First Agricultural Bank go to City Hall too.

George Nixon Briggs

Back on the South side a start-up company rents a room next to the empty bank building. It is 1851. George Nixon Briggs, a self-educated lawyer and former Governor, spots a niche for insurance and founds Berkshire Life Insurance Company. Benjamin F. Johnson of Pittsfield, Secretary-Treasurer of the new company, is the first policy holder.

Courtesy of The Berkshire Historical Society

Thomas F. Plunkett

Berkshire Life is an immediate success and Briggs soon moves to larger space on the second floor of Union Federal Savings Bank on North Street. Briggs is President until his death, ten years later, in 1861. He has named his Vice President to be his successor.

Thomas Fitzpatrick Plunkett, the new President, starts a dynasty in Berkshire Life which continues for 50 years until 1911. Under Plunkett's tenure the company continues its pattern of growth.

In 1868, Plunkett has the vision to put down corporate roots, across from Park Square.

The handsome building on the corner of North and West Streets is home to Berkshire Life for over 90 years.

The home of Berkshire Life Insurance Company, 1868

Courtesy of Berkshire Athenaeum

Initially insurance is primarily used to pay for funerals. It's a rough business. If a payment is late the policy gets lapsed and sold at an auction to the highest bidder. Berkshire Life is the first company to stop lapsing policies for non-payment. That is the start of Berkshire Life's ongoing reputation for innovation and honesty towards policy holders--and a key step toward making insurance an important factor in the economic structure of the country.

The new home office of Berkshire Life Insurance Company of America

Courtesy of Berkshire Life Insurnace

In 1958, Berkshire Life moves down Route 7 to a magnificent colonial building rising majestically on South Street. In 2004, in line with major industry changes, it merges with Guardian Life, a match of values and scale.

The Plunkett family leads Berkshire Life into the 20th Century. During his career Thomas Fitzpatrick is also Sr. Partner at Plunkett-Wyllys, a successful cotton manufacturer started by his Father. Following in Thomas F.'s footsteps, his son, William Robinson, leads Berkshire Life into its most successful period. Like his Father, he, too, is involved with textiles. Walk around Pittsfield and you'll keep coming across the Plunkett name, literally a pillar of the town. You can still cross paths with the Pittsfield Plunketts, a caring family with many fascinating branches.

Courtesy of Helen & Tom Plunkett

Thomas Fitzpatrick Plunkett

Courtesy of Helen & Tom Plunkett

William Robinson Plunkett

In 1853 on Water Street, on the banks of the Housatonic, Pittsfield Coal Gas starts. Thomas F. Plunkett, who will ultimately lead Berkshire Life, is the company's first President. The new coal gas brings a fresh sparkle and clarity of gas-lights to the business district as well as homes around town. The company is an immediate success.

Courtesy of Helen & Tom Plunkett

W.R.Plunkett's family

Pittsfield Coal Gas Company *Courtesy of Berkshire Gas*

In 1922 they change to water gas, a more environmentally friendly product, and ultimately to natural gas. In 1954 the name is changed to Berkshire Gas. After 153 years the company continues to be an integral part of Pittsfield life today, and their colorful logo is a familiar sight on a busy part of Rt. 8 and Cheshire Road.

Park Square, c. 1830 *Courtesy of The Berkshire Historical Society*

But let's go back to Park Square, which the service industries helped to develop. An historical presence on the Square is the Berkshire Medical Institution. Even though it is Pittsfield's most important school, it struggles financially for years. Its location next to the town cemetery creates a major controversy as families discover "loved ones" missing from their graves. In l867 the Med School closes. This makes two buildings vacant on prime real estate—and becomes the cue for a couple of wealthy cousins to consider a possible venture on Park Square that will benefit the town.

Thomas Allen, a millionaire, and Phinehas Allen, Jr., whose father started The Pittsfield Sun, know the free library needs more space.

Thomas Allen *Courtesy of The Berkshire Historical Society*

In 1850 The Pittsfield Library Association, starts with 800 volumes. Twenty years later when the legislature changes the name to the Berkshire Athenaeum the collection has grown to 2400 books.

Enter the two cousins: Thomas and Phinehas. They put their heads and their wallets together and reach an agreement with the town to fund a library. They have definite ideas about how their money is used, including the location and the look. The deal goes through in 1876-- and what a library they build!

Phinehas Allen, Jr. *Courtesy of The Berkshire Historical Society*

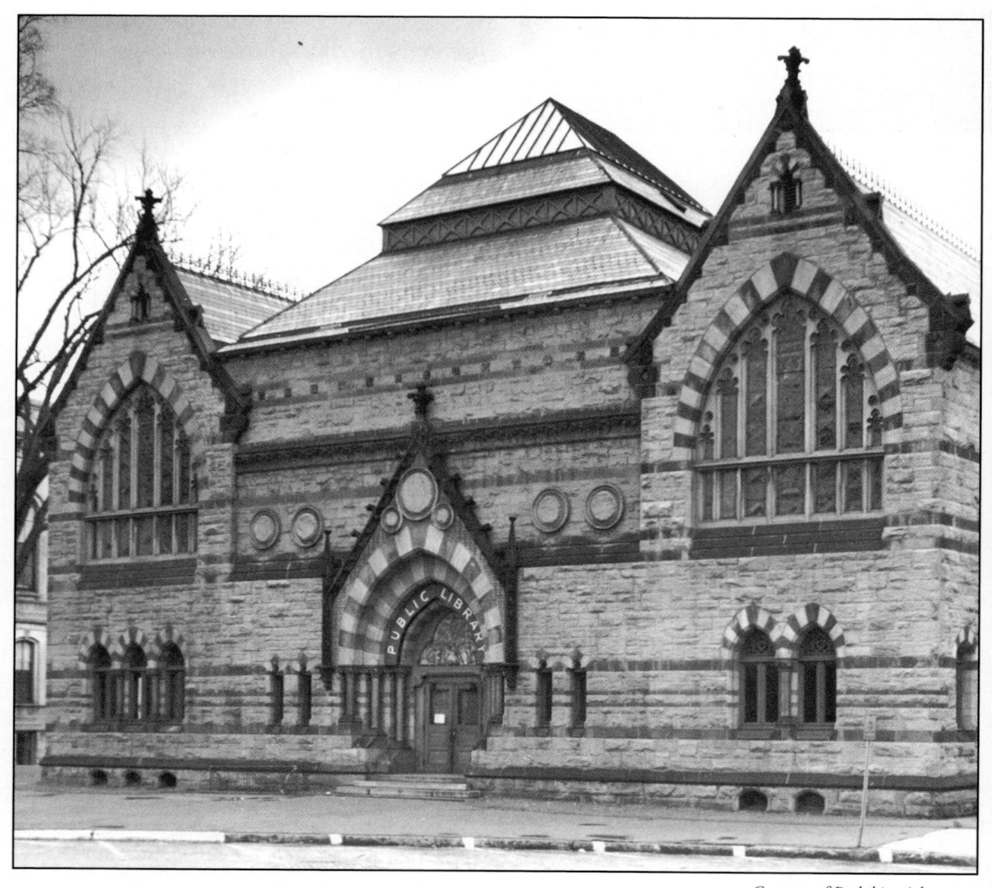

Courtesy of Berkshire Athenaeum

The original Berkshire Athenaeum 1876

You might say it presides on the South side of Park Square. A magnificent Gothic building that sort of looks like it anchors the city. Made of contrasting blue limestone with elegant Gothic windows on each side. **You can't miss it. And shouldn't.**

1860 - 1898

1860
- Octagon House built

1861
- Thomas F. Plunkett named President of Berkshire Life. Starts dynasty in insurance lasting 50 years

1862
- H. Davis & Co., department store, opens on North Street
- Rev. Samuel Harrison leaves church to work with the Abolitionist, Frederick Douglass. Soon appointed Chaplain of 54th Massachusetts Regiment of Black troops

1863
- Berkshire Medical School closes
- Council votes to find new ground for town cemetery

1865
- American House opens on North Street and Columbus. First hotel away from Park Square
- Pittsfield Elm Tree cut down: 340 years old, 128-feet tall
- Civil War ends

1868
- Berkshire Life Insurance moves to new corporate headquarters on West and North Streets. Stays 90-years

1869
- Temple Anshe Amunim founded. Second oldest Reform Congregation in the U.S.

1870
- Legislature changes library name to Berkshire Athenaeum: now has 2400 books

1871
- Burbank House built on North Street

1872
- Academy of Music opens
- Rev. Samuel Harrison returns to Pittsfield and Second Congregational Church
- Pleasure Park opens, a sportsman's delight. Today Deming Park

1874
- House of Mercy Hospital opens

1875
- Nesbit family businesses start. Nesbit Grocery, 3 Brother's Coal Co., Nesbit Garage and the Keator Group, spanning 130 years. Family still in town. Still in business.

1876
- The Allen cousins build the Berkshire Athenaeum on the South side of Park Square

1879
- Crane & Co. wins Government bid to produce U.S. bank note paper

1880
- Terry Clock Company formed
- Wood Brothers opens and sells musical instruments on North Street for 103 years

1881
- The Coliseum skating rink opens on Maplewood Avenue
- Grand Central Block opens. Name changes to Central Block. Still on North Street

1885
- William Stanley lights up North Street for Christmas
- A.H. Rice opens manufacturing facility to produce silk thread

1887
- Charles E. Hibbard moves his law firm to Pittsfield

1889
- Charter issued to The Co-op Bank

1890
- Council revises Charter and Pittsfield becomes a city
- Charles E. Hibbard elected first Mayor
- Stanley Electrical Manufacturing Company starts on Renne Avenue
- Abraham Burbank bequeaths money to develop city parks
- Burbank Park opens on Onota Lake

1891
- Kelton Miller buys weekly newspaper and starts a dynasty in publishing
- First trolley line built from depot to Pontoosuc Lake

1892
- George Burbank builds Wahconah Stadium

1893
- City Savings Bank opens on North Street
- Congregation Knesset Israel Synagogue organized
- Howard & Morrow open farm supply store on North Street

1895
- Elementary Schools open on Pontoosuc, Fenn, Orchard and other streets around town
- Charles L. Hibbard joins Father's firm

1896
- Pittsfield Cricket and Social Club organizes
- First Pittsfield High School opens on The Common for 600 students

1897
- Wealthy golfers organize 9-hole golf course between Williams Street and Dawes Avenue
- St. Joseph's School opens, first Parochial School in the city

1898
- Samuel and Carter Bowerman open elegant Wendell Hotel to honor their Father. Today, the Crowne Plaza on same site.
- Miss Hall's School for Girls officially founded
- Burgner's Farm starts delivering fresh food from the farm

BUT WHAT COMES NATURALLY WITH PITTSFIELD IS SPORTS...

Playing ball is engrained in the lives of Pittsfield children. Even with the Meeting House by-law.

This portrait of a young boy wearing his best vest and britches and clutching his baseball bat says it all.

Photograph: S.S. Wheeler

Courtesy of The Berkshire Historical Society

As factories and mills keep increasing, baseball becomes even more a part of the worker's lives. Teams are organized sponsored by the companies the players work for. Leagues are not far behind. When you go to the Crane & Company museum be sure to look for the picture of a Crane mill team in uniform.

By mid-19th century, baseball is a "gentleman's game", too. A sport which, like fraternities, singing clubs and gymnasiums develops traits of the "true gentleman".

The Pittsfield Baseball Club opens in 1840. Organized on a rather grand scale it has a playing field and meeting rooms. Some years later, in 1859, the Club hosts the first Intercollegiate Baseball Game between Amherst and Williams, in many ways a double-header: They play baseball and chess. "Muscle and Mind!"

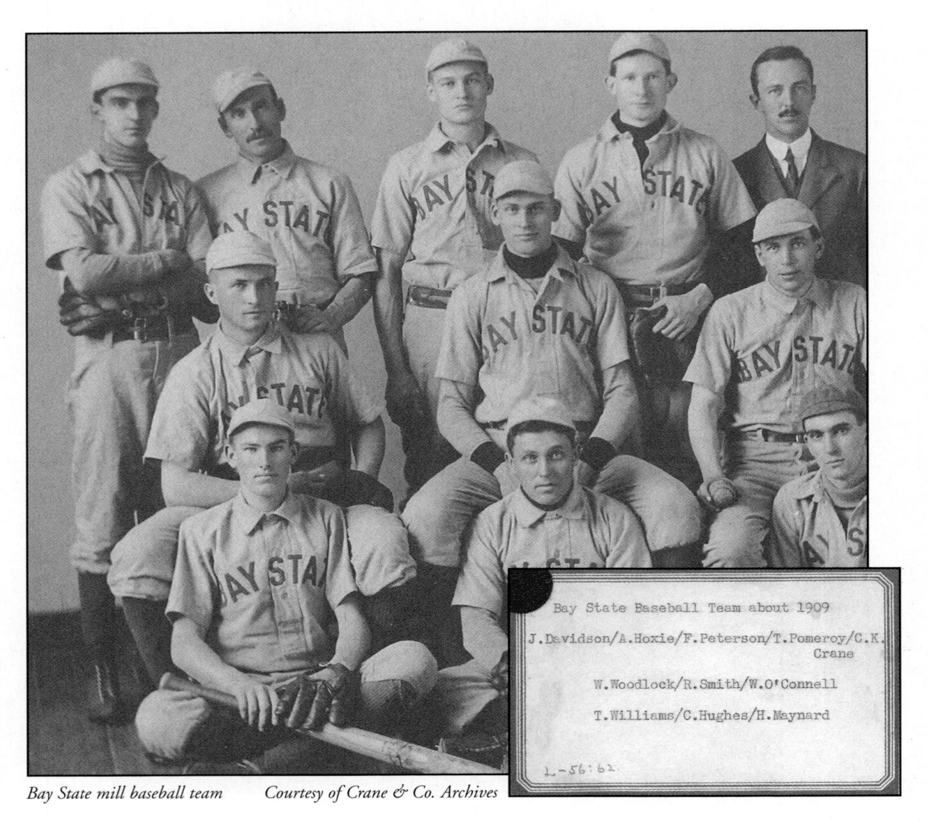

Bay State Baseball Team about 1909
J.Davidson/A.Hoxie/F.Peterson/T.Pomeroy/C.K. Crane
W.Woodlock/R.Smith/W.O'Connell
T.Williams/C.Hughes/H.Maynard

Bay State mill baseball team *Courtesy of Crane & Co. Archives*

Pittsfield sports facilities are growing in popularity and expansiveness.

In 1872 Pleasure Park opens. A true sportsman's delight, it has a baseball diamond, stables for riding horses, a track for horse-racing, and later on for bikes and cars and, of course, a glamorous club house. You can still play ball on this location on Newell Street, only now it is simpler and named Deming Park.

Across town on Maplewood Avenue off North Street, the Coliseum is built for roller skating. A mammoth wooden structure, it is the largest public space here and becomes the regular venue for the annual town meeting.

Photograph: Edwin Hale Lincoln

Burbank Park at Lake Onota *Courtesy of The Berkshire Historical Society*

Some years later, in 1890, a charming little park with flowering trees opens on Lake Onota. It is named for Abraham Burbank, a realtor and builder who, with his sons, builds a slew of multi-use buildings: houses, schools, hotels, generally in the center of town. A random list is: West's Block, Berkshire House, A.H. Rice Silk Mill. Burbank literally develops the look of Pittsfield. Abraham Burbank, raised in poverty, dies a millionaire in 1887 at the age of 72.

Photograph: Phyllis Kerle

Deming Park playground

Burbank leaves a bequest in his will to establish a system of town parks for recreational use--so kids and parents from all walks of life can toss a basketball, a baseball, hit a tennis ball or jog. Free.

Abraham Burbank is a man of vision, money and great compassion. He leaves his mark in Pittsfield for generations to enjoy.

Abraham Burbank *Courtesy of Kelton Burbank*

George Burbank, Abraham's son, fought in the Civil War with the 8th Massachusetts Volunteer Infantry and was taken prisoner. But he returns to Pittsfield and, like his father, is a builder and a sports enthusiast. He too sees a need in town: a ballpark. Going to a game at the Fair Grounds, now Springside Park, means a long walk and trolley ride. And Pittsfielders go to a lot of ball games!

So in 1892 George uses his own property to build a legendary athletic park on Wahconah Street. The stadium is accessible and good for all kinds of ball games. It also has tracks for bike races, jumping hurdles and running. In the 1920's, a player for the Hartford Senators hits a home run into the adjoining Housatonic River. His name? Lou Gehrig.

Photograph: Phyllis Kerle

The owls and the fans at Wahconah Park

Today Wahconah Park is a landmark stadium, complete with hanging stuffed owls to keep birds away. A treasure. With a little luck, you may catch a game at Wahconah...it's just down the road from the hospital.

You can still meet up with the fifth generation of Burbank's in Pittsfield. They have a history of civic responsibility and they care. It is no surprise that the Burbank name appears in law, on the City Council, Water Commissioner...they keep getting involved. This is a family the city can salute--with reason.

And what about golf in the 19th century?

The first 9-hole golf course is laid out in 1897 between Dawes Avenue and Williams Street for some wealthy enthusiasts. But the golfers have grand ideas and money. They soon take their passion to rolling greens on South Street and an elegant clubhouse with a history. How this becomes the Country Club of Pittsfield is another legend from the 19th century.

In 1781 Henry Van Schaack, a well-to-do Tory, literally run out of New York, moves to Pittsfield to recoup his reputation. He builds a gracious Dutch Colonial mansion with breathtaking views. This is the property Elkanah Watson buys for his model farm. Then Thomas Melville, Herman's uncle buys it and names it Broadhall. It is here while visiting that the young Herman is captivated by the mountains. Years later on the back of his uncle's property he has his own little home, complete with "views", once a busy inn on Holmes road. Today, Herman's house is home to the Berkshire Historical Society, and named Arrowhead for the arrowheads found in the ground. This is where he writes Moby Dick.

Courtesy of The Berkshire Historical Society

Greylock as Herman saw it.

The Country Club of Pittsfield today

Arrowhead

Photograph: Phyllis Kerle

Broadhall, the mansion on South Street which adjoins Herman's property, continues to make history. Ultimately the Melvilles, sell it to Sarah Morewood, a literary socialite. Her lively parties are famous with names like John Jay, Frederick Church and Oliver Wendell Holmes regularly crossing her threshold.

In 1900 another era begins. Sarah has died and her heirs sell the mansion to the golfers who take pride in their Clubhouse with a heritage.

As you drive North on Route 7 watch for the Country Club of Pittsfield. Imagine a quiet little lake in the middle of the golf course, Morewood Lake, named after the fascinating Sarah.

Courtesy of The Berkshire Historical Society

Sarah Morewood and children.

So men of vision keep the town moving forward, men whose family names, are still around as you'll see when you look up at the street signs.

The Persips, c. 1890

Courtesy of Eleanor Persip

W.R.Plunkett's family c. 1890

Courtesy of Helen & Tom Plunkett

BY THE TIME PITTSFIELD IS A TOWN, 1761, A TAVERN IS UP AND RUNNING...

Pittsfield has a heritage of people coming and going.

People come to Pittsfield for business, vacations, a stopping-point between cities...and everyone wants a place to stay.

Known to be a liberal city, it attracts men like Henry Van Schaack, the Tory of mansion fame, who escaped from NY in hopes of regaining his reputation. At times Pittsfield is a military depot and a local trading center. Soldiers, farmers and traders regularly come and go and everyone needs to eat and sleep.

Courtesy of Berkshire Athenaeum

Herman Melville

Captain David Bush operates Bush & Sons, a tavern on Holmes Road. The road is easy for travelers to find and it offers views of the mountains, always a Pittsfield draw. It is this little building that Herman Melville buys for his home some fifty years later, and which visitors now know as Arrowhead. He spends summers here and his children love the farm. Then in 1770 Captain John Strong builds a tavern on East and Bartlett on the site of Bishop Worthington's house (which Lemuel Pomeroy buys in 1800). Over on Depot and North Streets Ingersoll Tavern opens. It is here in 1786 where men captured during Shay's Rebellion are imprisoned. In 1796, one of the first "resorts", Goodrich Tavern, named for its proprietor, Jesse Goodrich, opens. Inns and taverns are popping up all around town. **You might say they set the tone of the city: comfortable, enjoyable, social.**

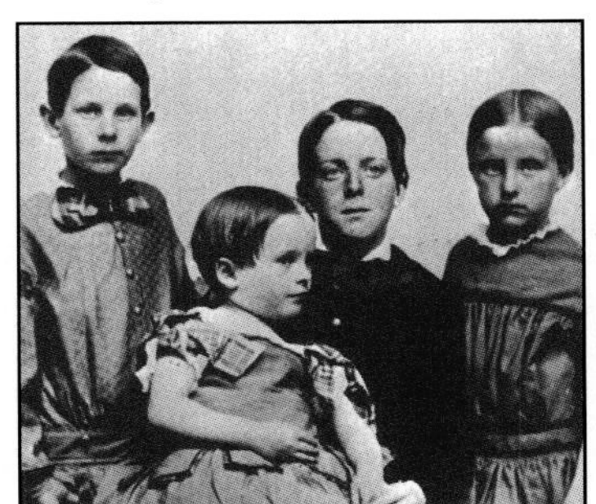

Courtesy of Berkshire Athenaeum

Herman Melville's children

Herman Melville's farm, Arrowhead

Courtesy of The Berkshire Historical Society

In 1798, across from Park Square, the American Hotel is started with Captain John Dickinson, Proprietor. That hotel changes hands frequently and in 1800 becomes the William Clark Hotel. Captain Joseph Merrick is the landlord. Merrick is a hard-nosed Republican who refuses to serve Federalists. That leads to an enterprising deal between the Federalists and the famous Reverend Thomas Allen, who still has some of the original lots given to him at his ordination. He sells them to the Federalists and in 1808 they build Pittsfield House on Park Square. In 1810 Simeon Griswold opens another hotel on Park Square and advertises "airy and convenient" rooms. It thrives for twenty years and then is sold to the Berkshire Medical Institution. **Nearby on Bank Row, in 1812, Campbell's Coffee House opens, and becomes a popular resort with British Officers. Today it's Patrick's Pub, a town favorite.**

The Wendell Hotel under construction

Courtesy of The Berkshire Historical Society

Wendell Hotel *Courtesy of Berkshire Athenaeum*

Merrick's Inn burns in 1826 and the property is eventually sold to the Berkshire Life Insurance Company for their home office. Across the street, on South and West Streets, James Colt builds a stately home which will eventually be converted to a hotel. The first, in 1846, is the Exchange Hotel, then the U.S. Hotel and, in 1898, Carter and Samuel Bowerman buy the property and open the luxurious Wendell Hotel as a tribute to their Father, whose law office was on that site. The elegant rooms, the services, the fresh flowers, the superb kitchen are all a reflection of the lifestyle of Samuel Bowerman, Sr. It continues as an upscale hotel to this day, only now it is the Crowne Plaza.

Obviously, while banks in Pittsfield move, hotels here change their names.

In 1860 on a landmark corner of Columbus Avenue and North Street, an old tavern is rebuilt and enlarged to become America House, the first hotel built away from Park Square. In 1871, Abraham Burbank, again with his visionary approach, opens Burbank House on North Street. **True to his philosophy he builds, "in the center of town" one of the first hotels to open away from Park Square, catering to business travelers and visitors coming for summer vacations.** Burbank House is well furnished, comfortable, with outstanding services and special amenities such as furniture handmade by Pittsfield artisans. The hotel is immediately successful, but the family keeps it only a few years.

Burbank House *Courtesy of Berkshire Athenaeum*

Some blocks away, on Wendell Avenue, Colonel Walter Cutting, newly retired from the military and accustomed to the finer things in life builds a magnificent 28-room mansion with a ball room. It is circa 1870 and this very rich, relative new-comer to Pittsfield who is a true bon-vivant, uses his mansion for lavish dinners, cotillions, dances and receptions. Almost thirty years later it is sold to two sisters, the Misses Henrietta and Alice Learned, who change the name and identity. The White Tree Inn becomes a classy rooming house which the sisters manage for almost forty years. A socially prominent venue for weddings, anniversary parties, dinners—very much in the style of Colonel Cutting.

Courtesy of Berkshire Athenaeum

The White Tree Inn

The era of the B&B is hovering on the horizon. An important and fun part of the Pittsfield scene, capturing the feeling of the old city mingling with the new. A treasure for visitors and locals.

Sarah Morewood and children c. 1860

Courtesy of The Berkshire Historical Society

Herman Melville's children, c. 1860

Courtesy of Berkshire Athenaeum

A BLOCK AWAY FROM PARK SQUARE, COMMERCE AND CULTURE ARE THRIVING ON NORTH STREET...

Here you can find a blacksmith, factories, places to eat, buy clothes, and see a show. One after the other on both sides of the street.

The broad expanse and bustle of North Street is likened to European boulevards. With a diverse array of businesses, all framed by multi-use buildings. Exciting architecture, far ahead of it's time.

West's Block *Courtesy of The Berkshire Historical Society*

West's Block, which opens in 1850 has shops and businesses on the first floor and upstairs, a large theatre. Some twenty years later, The Academy of Music is built with shops and businesses on the street level and upstairs, an even larger hall for diversified theatrical productions plus a classy restaurant. A few doors away, in 1881, Grand Central Block takes its position on the street with specialty shops, offices and, again, a large auditorium upstairs. Tenants shorten the name to Central Block which is easier to remember. Today a renovated version is on the same site, with the same shorter name.

North Street, c. 1855 *Courtesy of The Berkshire Historical Society*

In 1885, an electrical engineer, William Stanley, hangs Thomas Edison's incandescent lamps on the F.A. Robbins Jewelry Store, literally lighting up the street for Christmas, and dazzling shoppers.

William Stanley , c. 1915 Courtesy of The Berkshire Historical Society

Stanley is then hired by The Pittsfield Illuminating Company, and in 1890 he starts the Stanley Electrical Manufacturing Company. Working in a little building on Renne Avenue and Eagle Street, Stanley and his colleagues develop electrical transformers--and transform the electrical industry. In 1903 General Electric buys this small business. The rest is what legends are built on. It is interesting to note that many of the original incorporators and shareholders of the Stanley company are Pittsfield natives--investors in the "unknown"— families whose descendants still live in town.

General Electric 1903 *Courtesy of The Berkshire Historical Society*

And so, the skilled engineers from Stanley's company become part of The General Electric Corporation. Over the years, GE changes its core business and expands into new areas like electronic military control systems and ultimately GE Plastics. Along the way, the defense business of GE is purchased by Martin Marietta and Lockheed Martin and is sold to what is currently General Dynamics Advanced Information Systems on Plastics Avenue.

GDAIS is part of General Dynamics Corporation, one of the top five defense contractors worldwide. Here the company builds command and control systems for the U.S. Navy--utilizing Pittsfield's innovative skills developed over the last century.

When you walk along North Street, you might take a right on Fenn and go down to Renne Avenue, a quiet block where it's easy to stop the clock and imagine the sheer energy generated by the formidable William Stanley and his colleagues. Engineers whose descendants are today a part of General Dynamics. And while you are in this neighborhood, stop by the Lichtenstein Art Center, where a more visible creativity blossoms today.

North Street, c. 1860 Courtesy of The Berkshire Historical Society

Nearby is Eagle Street, where legends are literally printed. In 1891, Kelton Miller buys The Weekly Eagle newspaper and starts a dynasty in publishing and a unique paper.

Courtesy of Mark Miller and The Berkshire Eagle

The Millers: Kelton, Lawrence (Pete) and Donald

A year later, the Weekly Eagle becomes a daily and soon after joins the Associated Press. In 1904 the Eagle moves to its own elegant flatiron building. Then in the late 30's, Kelton's sons take over: Donald becomes publisher and Lawrence (Pete) editor. They create a publication with an attitude that welcomes outspoken opinions and ultimately brings a Pulitzer Prize, top reporters, and a reputation as a training ground. Pete's sons, Michael and Mark go one step further and print a Sunday edition.

It has been "reported" that The Eagle is comparable to The New York Times on a local level. The Miller mission has been unwavering: Make an interesting paper. If profits come along, "fantastic". In 1995, The Berkshire Eagle and the family part company.

Eagle Publishing Company composing room, c. 1900 *Courtesy of The Berkshire Historical Society*

The third generation of Millers continue to live in Pittsfield—and you can still run into the family at The Soda Chef, a popular meeting spot on North Street.

Business and banking continue to grow during the 1890's. A charter is granted to The CO-OP Bank in 1889 and it opens in Kookes Banking House, on North Street. A community-oriented bank, it takes a fresh approach to the business and focuses on the average citizen, encouraging them to open savings accounts and develop systematic payments for home mortgages. It sort of reflects the thrifty spirit of the city. Now the home office is on South Street, where the CO-OP continues to quietly encourage community responsibility with employees and officers via unique Children's Saving Programs and Scholarship Programs. **A friend to many.**

Pittsfield takes a major step forward in 1890.

The charter is revised and after forty years, the town becomes a city with an elected mayor.

Courtesy of Cain Hibbard Myers & Cook

Charles E. Hibbard

Charles E. Hibbard is the first to hold office. The charter vote is very close and leaders of both parties are determined to select a man with an impeccable reputation. Hibbard, a Democrat, is a distinguished lawyer, a brilliant litigator, and...has never been involved in town government. The perfect candidate. Admitted to the Massachusetts Bar in 1869, he moves his law firm to Pittsfield in 1887, and that same year, is elected District Attorney. He is also one of the incorporators of the Stanley Electric Company, and ultimately becomes President of the Massachusetts Bar. **It has been said that Hibbard started a family whose impact on the growth of Pittsfield is beyond measure.**

Courtesy of Cain Hibbard Myers & Cook

Charles L. Hibbard

Hibbard's son, Charles L., joins his Father in 1895. A member of the Judiciary for 48 years, Charles is considered one of Pittsfield's greatest public servants. His grandson, Stephen, becomes the third generation of Hibbard lawyers, and the name is still in a law firm on West Street. **Roots go deep in Pittsfield.**

Courtesy of Cain Hibbard Myers & Cook

Stephen B. Hibbard

Now that Pittsfield is a city, there is reason for a namesake bank and in 1893, City Savings Bank arrives on North Street. A major financial institution, it is the dream of twenty-five Pittsfield citizens who pledge their own money to create a savings bank, exclusively for Berkshire County citizens. The first deposit of $1000 is made by James A. Burbank. City Savings, now Legacy Bank, crisscrosses North Street over a period of years and eventually builds a superb financial center. North Street is always home to this local institution.

Shaker School, c. 1880 *Courtesy of The Berkshire Historical Society*

The five Nesbit brothers: Robert, George Washington, Basil, Leo and William, c. 1920 *Courtesy of David Keator*

Courtesy of The Berkshire Eagle

England Brothers and Sales Associates

Courtesy of The Berkshire Historical Society

Thaddeus Clapp House, c. 1880 on Wendell Avenue

Familiar names around town...

All Photographs: Phyllis Kerle

1900 - 2006

1900
- Golfers buy Broadhall Mansion from the Morewood family. Golf moves to South Street and the Country Club of Pittsfield is started.
- J.M. Holmes Secretarial School opens on North Street
- Cooper's Coal opens...Hot Stuff
- Reverend Samuel Harrison dies

1903
- The General Electric Corporation buys Stanley Electrical Manufacturing Company
- Zenas Crane Jr. opens Berkshire Museum of Art and Natural History
- The curtain goes up at the Colonial Theatre

1904
- The Berkshire Eagle moves to Flatiron Building

1909
- YMCA opens
- Miss Hall's School moves to Holmes Road

1912
- Union Square Theatre opens. Soon named The Music Hall

1914
- Electric lights strung on Park Square Christmas Tree
- Harry's market opens on Wahconah Street. Still at same location. Now there are two Harry's plus a package store in town. Nichols family still the owner

1916
- Elizabeth Sprague Coolidge holds chamber music groups in her home on West Street

1918
- Coolidge Chamber Groups expand to South Mountain Concerts. Still playing in their own Concert Hall

1924
- Lou Gehrig hits home run from Wahconah Park into Housatonic River

1925
- W.T. Grant opens on North Street. Stays 44-years
- O'Connell Oil starts. Still carrying on the tradition

1926
- Puritan Bar/Restaurant opens on North Street. Today: The Lantern. Still going strong

1931
- New Pittsfield High School opens on East Street. One of the largest schools in New England

1932
- GE Plastics comes to Pittsfield

1936
- Petricca Construction Co., starts. Today, a unique Pittsfield landmark business known around the world for pre-cast concrete bridge components

1937
- GE Credit Union organized

1938
- WBRK, Pittsfield's first radio station, starts broadcasting

1940
- Winnie Davis Crane founds the Pittsfield Community Music School. Now: The Berkshire Music School on Wendell Avenue

1946
- The Berkshire Eagle starts WBEC and Pittsfield has two radio stations

1958
- Berkshire Life Insurance moves to new Colonial Building on South Street

1960
- Last Shakers at Hancock Village

1964
- First Hallowe'en Parade on North Street
- Quality Printing moves to town

1969
- Taconic High School opens. Comprehensive curriculum for 1150 students.

1971
- WBRG AM/FM appears as "alternative" radio
- West Side Clock Shop starts ticking on North Street

1977
- WUPE/WHOOPEE takes over when WBRG is sold. An eclectic radio programmer goes on the air

1979
- Guido's opens and "fresh" takes on new meaning

1980
- Berkshire Alarms starts to protect Pittsfield

1981
- 10th Ethnic Fair. 12,000 attend

1983
- Persip Day celebrated
- Paul Rich Home Furnishings opens on North Street
- Steve Valenti Men's Clothing store opens too

1988
- England Brothers closes its doors

1995
- Greylock Credit Union receives Federal Charter. (Formerly General Electric Credit Union)

1996
- General Dynamics Advanced Information Systems opens offices on Plastics Avenue

1998
- England Brothers building demolished. Legacy Bank goes up

2002
- Storefront Artist Project launched

2004
- Sheeptacular takes over the city
- Lichtenstein Art Center opens on Renne Avenue
- Joseph Scelsi Intermodal Transportation Center opens. Honors former Mayor and Councilman

2005
- First Pittsfield Jazz Festival
- Barrington Stage buys Music Hall and moves to Pittsfield

2006
- The Gilded Age in Pittsfield exhibit opens at Arrowhead
- Art of the Game Baseball exhibit starts 2-yr show
- Interprint opens new facility
- Ethnic Fair in the works

AND WHAT KEEPS THE DAY-TO-DAY TRAFFIC HUMMING ON NORTH STREET? RETAILERS!

What else?

A legend in his own right: Moses England, a Bavarian immigrant. England is born with retailing in his blood, and he passes it on to his sons.

Moses instinctively chooses North Street for his first store in 1857. Then in 1891 he crosses the street to Newman's Block and opens a store that keeps expanding and becomes a retailing institution. His benchmark: quality, service and...excitement. The towering ceilings take everyone by surprise.

Moses England *Courtesy of The Berkshire Eagle*

Every December the Christmas tree at England Brothers seems to grow into the sky! His three sons continue the legacy, year after year, making England Brothers the leading department store in Berkshire County, with roots firmly placed on North Street.

Celebrating 100 Years *Courtesy of The Berkshire Eagle*

As the 21st century draws to a close in 1988, after more than a century making retailing memories and friends England Brothers closes its doors, and an era ends.

Around the same time that Moses England opens his store, another department store starts under the name of H.G. Davis & Co. It is 1862 and it eventually becomes a landmark specialty shop named Holden & Stone. This sophisticated store is a forerunner of its time, championing a shorter work week and longer vacations for employees. **A little known story is that Marshall Field gets his foot into the retailing door here on North Street before moving on to bigger things in Chicago.** The name changes frequently over the years and the store eventually moves to Central Block, the "right" side of North Street. It continues in business until 1944.

Howard & Morrow, c. 1893 Courtesy of The Berkshire Historical Society

Other landmark names with strong bases on North Street are W.T. Grant in business over forty years from 1925-1969. Wood Brothers, a unique store selling all kinds of musical instruments open their doors in 1880. The store is a fun presence until 1983, when they move to Allendale. Howard & Morrow, 59 North Street, a phenomenal resource to farmers, starts in 1893. The store operates until 1960, the last years under Frank Howard's name--and until farms around here start to disappear.

Coopers Coal Courtesy of The Berkshire Historical Society

1900--and things are heating up. Coopers Coal "Hot Stuff" opens on North Street. Coal and wood for the town, taking care of cooking and heating. Also in 1900, another career opportunity appears: a secretarial school, Berkshire Business College & School of Shorthand, operated by J.M. Holmes. Ads promise "competent help" supplied to offices. In 1909, the YMCA makes its presence known in the downtown area.

Berkshire Business College & School of Shorthand, c. 1900

One of the ongoing characteristics of North Street is upscale retailers. Paul Rich Home Furnishings, since 1983, has attracted clients who come from all over the country. The dapper founder whose name is a household word around town is known to guide the most inexperienced or the most sophisticated shopper to a new "look" at home, or a makeover that will please people who live here or visit. Paul Rich continues to be a family-owned business, and the second generation is now leading the store. Recently they bought the building--a commitment to North Street and Pittsfield. The Rich family mission is clear-cut, their tasteful point of view a welcome influence.

North Street, c. 1911 *Courtesy of Berkshire Athenaeum*

Another retailer on North Street who brings a touch of class to the neighborhood is Steve Valenti, the men's clothing store. Steve dresses locals and visitors, the known and unknown and he makes the whole process fun and enjoyable. Steve has an unbeatable reputation for service and sheer caring. Once you get to know this group, Valenti's becomes a place to stop by and pick up on what's happening in town.

Courtesy of The Berkshire Historical Society

North Street, 1850, the oldest photograph of the town

Today, North Street continues to be a key focus of the city with all kinds of fun, appealing shops and restaurants opening, a tribute to the city and its ongoing diversity.

WHEN THE SUN GOES DOWN, NORTH STREET REALLY LIGHTS UP...

And Pittsfield establishes its cultural interests early on.

West's Block gets the fun started in 1850, with productions the townspeople are eager to attend.

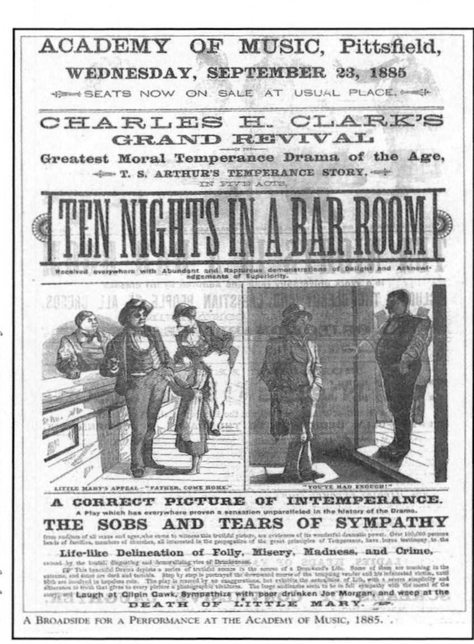

Courtesy of The Berkshire Historical Society

A broadsheet for The Academy of Music

It is The Music Academy, however, that steals the show almost as soon as it opens in 1872. This 1100 seat hall hosts symphony orchestras, chamber groups, vocal concerts, operas as well as literary readings, traveling theatrical players, and...animal acts. To round out the evening, attendees can dine at the Palais Royal, the Academy's glamorous restaurant. The Music Academy flourishes for thirty one years. By then, other stellar venues come to town.

In 1903 a major theatre opens on South Street. The Colonial Theatre is a visual gem and the premiere theatre of its era. The Colonial's superb productions are hard to match anywhere in the world. At its prime, John Barrymore and his sister Ethel, Sarah Bernhardt, the dancer Anna Pavlova, Lillian Russell and even the Ziegfeld Follies appear when the curtain goes up. Today plans are underway to restore this neo-classical treasure and keep the legend going.

The Colonial Theatre on South Street Courtesy of Berkshire Athenaeum

And in the busy year of 1903, Zenas Crane Jr., is making more things happen: He opens the Berkshire Museum of Art and Natural History. The new museum is spacious and elegant, perfect for the collections from the now crowded Berkshire Athenaeum. What's more, Zenas expands the museum and adds many rare pieces from his own travels continually treating lucky Pittsfield families to ongoing fascinations which enrich and add fun to their lives. A friend of Zenas', and a major help in organizing this remarkable institution, is William Robinson Plunkett. Both families help to keep the art and cultural scene expanding over the years.

Zenas Crane Jr. *Courtesy of Crane & Co. Archives*

In Pittsfield family names continue to criss-cross in various ventures that broaden the city's appeal.

Berkshire Museum of Art and Natural History *Courtesy of Berkshire Athenaeum*

There is more. In 1912 Union Square Theatre is built on Union Street. It eventually becomes The Music Hall. Over the years it hosts an incredible array of theatre, vaudeville, movies and other entertainments. Another architectural beauty, it too is being restored. **Then in 2005 Barrington Stage buys the building and brings to Pittsfield its award-winning productions: musicals, comedies, the classics, originals... an incredible and special mix of the old and the new. Plus...one more name change: Barrington Stage.**

Barrington Stage Company, Pittsfield's newest star

Further out in the spectacular Pittsfield hills in 1916 a woman of vision, Elizabeth Coolidge Sprague, starts a series of chamber music concerts, small musical soirées held in her home on West Street. They soon grow and in 1918 become The South Mountain Concerts. With her enthusiasm, standards of excellence and sheer determination, Elizabeth Sprague is known as The Fairy Godmother of Chamber Music. Her list of performers reads like a Who's Who of American Music in the 20th Century: Rudolph Serkin, Myra Hess, the Budapest String Quartet, and on and on. Sprague is another outsider who "discovers" Pittsfield and ultimately decides to live here. She builds a home on South Mountain, then a concert hall and finally cottages so the musicians can relax. Her concert hall is now in the National Register of Historic Places. Elizabeth Sprague and her husband are "home" here in the Pittsfield Cemetery.

South Mountain Concert Hall Courtesy of The Berkshire Historical Society

IN THE THIRTIES, PITTSFIELD TUNES INTO RADIO IN A BIG WAY...

Pittsfield follows the broadcast trend in the 30's.

It is 1938, a dozen years after broadcast radio sweeps the country. WBRK takes to the airwaves from two studios located on Bank Row.

An affiliate of CBS in New York City, the station is on the air every day from 7:00am-1:00am. They do some local programming but mostly it is rebroadcasts of national shows. The first network show: The Major Bowes Amateur Hour! WBRK uses six experienced announcers with two locals in training and a long line of would be broadcasters waiting for auditions.

The station concentrates on local news, weather reports, ski news-- and builds an audience quickly. From the beginning, WBRK has a pioneering spirit inaugurating educational programs in classrooms, religious broadcasts, forums with Boston University, even producing more than its required share of public service promotions.

Then in 1946, a radio permit is issued to the publishers of the Berkshire Eagle with unlimited hours of broadcasting, reaching a radius of 25 miles.

"Pete" Miller and his brother Donald are caught up in the excitement of this new medium and position it as a complement to the newspaper, pulling experienced people from one communicator to the other. WBEC (Berkshire Eagle) goes on the air in March 1947. They extend their publishing contracts with national news

WBEC in 1947 on Eagle Street *Courtesy of WUPE*

The Millers: Kelton, Lawrence (Pete) and Donald *Courtesy of Mark Miller and The Berkshire Eagle*

reports from the Associated Press, weather and local news prepared by their reporters, and even start a popular children's program on Saturdays. An ABC affiliate, WBEC broadcasts from the third floor of the Miller building on Eagle Street and quickly becomes a strong competitor to WBRK. However, The Miller family has publishing in their blood and in 1961, they sell WBEC and buy another newspaper in Bennington, Vermont.

WBEC moves in 1964 to Jason Street. Now WUPE calls it home, too *Courtesy of WUPE*

Radio continues to flourish in this reasonably small city. In 1971 another permit is issued for a Pittsfield station with AM and FM frequency: WGRG and WGRG-FM. Only this station, broadcasting from North Street, chooses to position itself as an "alternative" for a range of music formats with news commentaries, even astrology forecasts. The station soon wins awards, and listeners who consider themselves "progressive". WGRG's audience is loyal but the station is not making money. In 1977, it is sold. The new owner makes a bold move and changes the name to one that is pronounceable--and fun: WUPE. WHOOPEE...where programming is eclectic--and competitive. At first WUPE is fully automated, but in a few months management brings in live announcers at key times and warms up the ambience. WUPE has no network affiliation, but is on the air 24 hours a day and soon rises to the top.

So here is little Pittsfield, caught in a broadcast war--with three viable and essentially different radio stations--quality broadcasting, giving listeners outstanding choices with plenty of opportunities to switch the dial.

Skater, c. 1867 *Photograph: Elizabeth Jackson*

England Brothers celebrating the 4th of July

Courtesy of The Berkshire Historical Society

Sculpted moldings at the Colonial Theatre *Photograph: Phyllis Kerle*

Herman Melville

Courtesy of Berkshire Athenaeum

Holden & Stone delivery truck

The Pontoosuc Woolen Co. *Courtesy of Berkshire Athenaeum*

Pittsfield High School, c. 1898 — Courtesy of The Berkshire Historical Society

A popular season: Winter — Photograph: Phyllis Kerl

Courtesy of The Berkshire Historical Society

The Octagon House, Built 1860

Theodore Pomeroy and Laura, c. 1866

Pomeroy House, c. 1870

Holmesdale, c. 1910 — Courtesy of The Berkshire Historical Society

Photograph: S.S. Wheeler

Boating on Pontoosuc Lake, c. 1895 *Courtesy of The Berkshire Historical Society*

Thomas Allen House, 1880 *Courtesy of The Berkshire Historical Society*

The Plunkett School *Photograph: Phyllis Kerle*

Holmesdale today *Photograph: Phyllis Kerle*

Courtesy of Berkshire Athenaeum

First Baptist Church

A.H. Rice and Compnay Courtesy of The Berkshire Historical Society

Courtesy of Berkshire Athenaeum

Berkshire Life Insurnace Co. in 1878

Central Pittsfield, 1770 Courtesy of The Berkshire Historical Society

Allan Farm Gate Courtesy of The Berkshire Historical Society

Pontoosuc Lake, c. 1878 Courtesy of The Berkshire Historical Society

LIKE A PARTY? And...riding a bike, playing tennis, walking the hills, going to the theatre? In Pittsfield, we mix it up and end up with fun ideas that have a definite stamp of the area.

Here is a little change of pace: A few pages with tips on how-to-organize an activity followed by a get-together with menus and recipes. Some recipes come from local hosts/hostesses. Enjoying life comes with the territory in Pittsfield.

LIVING LEGENDS... THE PITTSFIELD ENTERTAINERS

Kind of a behind-the-scenes look at Pittsfield today.

Bike the rambling Ashuwillticook Trail or map your own route...

Interesting way to see the sights or explore back roads.
You want to choose low traffic roads with good cycle paths.

For a group of infrequent riders, plan a ride of 1-1-1/2 hours; experienced riders: 2-3 hours.

Watch for hills and scenic points. (This is the Berkshires!) Will you pass something like a Festival, a Fair, a Market? Work it in. A circle route or loop for the total ride is perfect planning.

What's the headcount? 8-12 cyclists is a manageable number. If some of your friends are serious riders, remind them ahead of time that this is a party, and some of the group may "ride the brakes".

Don't forget: Everyone brings water and a helmet. And have someone ride the route ahead of time. It helps to know where you are going.

A Tennis Round Robin keeps everyone moving...

Choose a spot with at least 2 courts you can reserve. Book them before you call your guests. And factor in a rain date. For 8-12 players, reserve 2 courts. Mix up the level of players, pretend you're at Wimbledon.

Players draw a number for partners: they play a set OR five games, then move on. You can pair winners against winners, men against women...there are no rules, just keep everyone playing. A prize adds to the fun. **Don't forget:** Extra balls, a score board with games, names, updated scores. And...everyone gets 10-20 minutes to warm up.

How to pack a sporty picnic

(not exactly an 18th century "small and hearty" but the same strategy, sort of...)

Lunch: Easy to serve salads, sandwiches/wraps players fix themselves.

Supper: Broiled chicken or salmon, cooked ahead of time and served at room temperature.

You can send out an SOS for large coolers and everything that goes in them is already cold. Ex. Salads in plastic bowls, butter, cheese. Or, tomatoes you slice when ready to serve. Food/beverages go in baskets, coolers or boxes. Flatware and table accessories in another. Everything has a post-it label. Colorful plastic plates, goblets, flutes add a classy "unbreakable" touch.

Don't forget: Candles, holders and matches if you're partying when the sun goes down. A folding serving table which acts like a buffet. Everyone brings his own chair/blanket/tray/folding table.

MENU

Picnic Lunch

- Juices/soda/water
- Iced Tea
- Bowls of crudités (no dip)
  - Cauliflower/apples/carrots
- Fix your own wraps and pitas:
  - Egg salad with chopped green or red pepper
  - Tuna fish with apple
  - Cream cheese with chutney
- Cookies OR go to a local soft serve

Sunset Supper

Prepared at home. Just serve.

- Water/wines/beer in coolers
- Broiled chicken legs with tarragon
- Broiled salmon fillets with lemon
- Baked beans*
- Potato salad*
- Bowls of grape tomatoes
- Lemon Squares

RECIPES

***Mom Persip's Legendary Baked Beans**

1 lb	dried navy or pea beans
6 c	water
1/2 lb	salt pork, cut into cubes
1	small onion
1/3 c	molasses
1/4 c	brown sugar
1/2 tsp	dry mustard
1/4 tsp	pepper

Soak beans overnight in water. Place (with soaking water) in large kettle. Add cold water and cover. Bring to boil; simmer until tender. Drain, reserve liquid. Place beans in 2-qt. pot. Combine molasses, sugar, mustard, onion and saltpork in a sauce pan and simmer 1/2 hr. Reserve liquid mixture. Pour over beans in pot--enough to cover beans. Cover pot and bake at 300° for 2 hrs. Add liquid if necessary and stir. Continue baking 1-1/2-2-hrs. longer until beans are tender. Bake uncovered for last 1/2-hr.

Eleanor Persip says:
"try them and understand why they are famous!"

***Mom Persip's Potato Salad Tip**

Marinate the potatoes in oil and vinegar dressing for 1-hr.

2-3 lbs	white or red cooked potatoes cut up/diced
1/4 c	chopped celery
2	eggs chopped
2 tbs	finely chopped onion
1 tsp	chopped parsley

Make your own oil and vinegar salad dressing. Or use Caesar salad bottled dressing. Mix all ingredients. Add rest of dressing, a little at a time. Stir. Chill.

A night at Barrington Stage...
The Colonial Theatre

This is one time you need to plan ahead. Once you choose a production, try to reserve a block of tickets. Most likely your guests will pay for their own tickets so it is considerate to reserve seats at different prices. If you reserve ahead of time, phone/email the cut-off date to accommodate the theatre. If you choose to put everything on one credit card, you'll want to give your guests a date for payment. That done, it's time to think about transportation. How about teaming up to go to the theatre after dinner?

Get the party off to a fun start with champagne or wine when your friends arrive. Think of leaving after the entree and coming back for dessert. If you take that route, you'll want to arrange for someone to clear the tables. Unless you can close a door.

Theatre is always a good excuse to "dress up" but just pass the word along. A written invitation helps to set the tone of your event. *Don't forget:* You want to enjoy your gathering. The less to do on "the" day, the more relaxed you'll be. Make lists. Look over your recipes and plan to prepare the food in steps. Try to set your table early in the week, put candles in place (with matches) and arrange flowers the day before.

Extra serving pieces are helpful (they don't have to match). Bring out your grandmother's platter or covered serving dish. Family heirlooms are a source of pride and keep conversation going.

MENU

Dinner

(With fresh salmon, vegetables and a pudding, the Villagers would feel they were at a lavish "5 o'clock dinner".)

- Pass or have ready to pour wines/beer/waters
- Bowl of nuts

Appetizers

- Hummus with pita triangles/chips
- Fresh shrimp with mixed sauces
- Celery and olives
- Gricini

Entrée

- Salmon fillets (broil with butter or margarine, freshly squeezed lemon)
- Sunday Ham*
- Saffron rice
- Cauliflower tossed with butter and a dash of curry powder
- Watercress and endive salad tossed in French Dressing

Dessert

- Cream Puffs*
- Grandma Smith's Classic Bread pudding*

RECIPES

*Sunday Ham

3-lb	pre-cooked ham
1-1 lb	can sour cherries (black)
1/4 c	brown sugar
3 tbs	brandy
1 tbs	dry mustard

Sauce:

Pour syrup from can of cherries into bowl. (Reserve cherries) Add mustard, stir until dissolved. Add brown sugar and brandy. Mix until smooth. One hour before serving, heat ham in moderate oven (375°). Make sauce; warm cherries in sauce. Serve individual portions, or slice ham, serve on platter. Put sauce and cherries in gravyboat.

A favorite of Katherine Benedett Lupoli

*Grandma Smith's Classic Bread Pudding

2 c	whole milk
4 c	cubed dried bread
1/2 c	granulated sugar
2	lightly beaten eggs
1 tsp	cinnamon or nutmeg
1/2 c	raisins

Preheat oven to 350°. Scald milk. Pour over cubes of bread in baking dish. Add other ingredients. Bake 20-25 min. Serve with ice cream or whipped cream. *Rebecca Smith*

Tip from Becky: use dried croissants instead of bread. Chocolate pieces instead of raisins.

*Cream Puffs

1/2 c	butter
1 c	water
1 c	flour
4	unbeaten eggs

Heat butter in water until butter is melted. Add flour. Stir vigorously until mixture no longer sticks to pan. Remove from stove. Cool slightly. Add eggs one at a time, beating after each egg is added. Drop by heaping tablespoons onto large greased cookie sheet, 2-in apart. Bake 20-min at 450°. Reduce heat to 425° Bake 20-min. Cool. Split. Fill with custard. Use packaged vanilla pudding flavored with 1 tbs Grand Marnier or: butterscotch pudding with 1 tsp nutmeg. *Phyllis Kerle*

And Then There is...THE HORS D'OEUVERIE

Finger foods that are easy to pass and nibble. A delicious way to keep people mingling and visit with your guests. A good rule of thumb for any party: invite someone new. A cool way to bring people together. Everyone wants to meet the new person and make him/her feel "at home".

MENU

Finger Foods

Hearty beginnings and middles.
(Leave some time between courses)

- Hummus dip with pita triangles or chips
- Smoked salmon on wheat crackers sprinkled with fresh pepper/lemon slices
- Stuffed eggs
- Cut up hard cheese on platter (Gouda/Cheddar/Appenzellar...)

- Slices of turkey breast on small rye slices spread with mustard or chutney
- Chicken salad in phyllo shells
- Thin slices of Chateaubriand or roast beef rolled

- Sweets: Grandma Hattie's Lemon Pound Cake
  Best Chocolate Cake from Pat's Mom

Chicken Salad With Melon

2 tbs	tarragon wine vinegar
2 tbs	minced fresh tarragon
3/4 tbs	salt
1/2 tbs	freshly ground pepper
1/4 c plus	2 tbs light olive oil
1/4 c	minced red onion
3 lbs	sauteed chicken breasts
1	medium cantaloupe cut in small pieces
	Phyllo shells

Season chicken breasts with salt and pepper. Heat 1/4 c olive oil over high heat in a large skillet. Add chicken. Brown 5-minutes, each side, until juices run clear. Cool. Cover. Refrigerate 1-2 days. In large bowl, combine vinegar, tarragon, salt, pepper, rest of oil. Cut chicken into bite-size pieces. Toss gently with onion and melon. Let sit 1/2 hour. Fill shells. *Ellen Ruberto*

Best Chocolate Cake from Pat's Mom

3 c	flour	12 tbs	vegetable oil
1 tsp	salt	2 tbs	vinegar
2 c	sugar	2 tbs	vanilla
2 tsp	baking soda	2 c	cold water
6 tbs	cocoa		

Preheat oven to 350°. Sift dry ingredients into loaf pan: 13x9x2. Poke 3 holes in these ingredients. Hole #1: Pour 12 tbs vegetable oil. #2: 2 tbs vinegar. #3: 2 tbs vanilla. Pour 2 c cold water over everything. Mix with fork until smooth. Bake at 350° 35-min. Touch center of cake. It springs up. *Pat Guthrie*

Grandma Hattie's Lemon Pound Cake

3 c	all purpose flour
2 c	sugar, less 1 tbs
3 tsp	baking powder
1 tsp	salt (Kosher is best)
4	large eggs
1 c	canola oil
1 c	1% milk
1-1/2	capfuls pure vanilla
	zest of one large lemon
	dried orange peel
	dried lemon peel
	cinnamon

Two 12"x 4" loaf pans. Coat well with non-stick/flour spray. Preheat oven to 375°. In large bowl, mix flour, sugar, baking powder, salt, dried lemon and orange peels, and cinnamon. Mix well with whisk. In smaller bowl, beat eggs lightly, add oil, then milk, stirring into eggs until blended. Add vanilla and zest lemon thoroughly over mixture. Stir together; combine with dry ingredients. Let stand 15-min. Pour batter equally into each pan. Sprinkle lightly with additional cinnamon. Put into heated oven for 5-min. Reduce heat to 350° and bake for 40-min. The loaves should be lightly browned. Test center with toothpick. Should come out dry. *Glaze:* In small skillet (aluminum best) combine juice from large lemon you zested, with 3 tbs unsweetened lemon juice and 1/2 c sugar. Stir until sugar is dissolved and you can see bottom of pan. Add some dried lemon and orange peels, continuing to stir until liquid bubbles. Let stand until cool. It thickens as it stands. When loaves are done and still in the pans, punch holes from top down, some all the way through, some part-way. Spoon glaze over loaves. Some will penetrate cake, some will coat it. Let cool in pans. Remove and continue to cool on a rack. Wrap in aluminum foil. Chill. *J. Peter Bergman*

21ST CENTURY

The legend continues...

IT IS ALMOST 300 YEARS SINCE...

SOLOMON DEMING moved his family to Poontoosuck, soon to be Pittsfield

LUCRETIA and **JOHN CHANDLER WILLIAMS** jumped into the Meeting House fracas--and helped to make Pittsfield a legend in baseball history

JOHN PERSIP, a black stowaway, started a landscaping business and a family which is still active in town

LEMUEL POMEROY got involved with the Council and ended up building a Town Hall and making room for St. Stephen's Episcopal Church

ARTHUR SCHOLFIELD brought his wool carding machine to town

PHINEHAS ALLEN started a newspaper

ZENAS CRANE built a paper mill

CHARLES HIBBARD was elected Mayor

GEORGE BRIGGS started an insurance company and **THOMAS PLUNKETT** started a dynasty in insurance that lasted fifty years

ABRAHAM BURBANK created a system of Free parks in Pittsfield and son George built Wahconah Park, a landmark stadium

Two cousins **THOMAS** and **PHINEHAS ALLEN** built the Berkshire Athenaeum

WILLIAM STANLEY took technology to new heights

KELTON MILLER started a publishing dynasty and a newspaper that still makes headlines

And...Pittsfield people continue to enjoy the natural environment along with an array of concerts, theatre, opera--a lifestyle of sports and culture that started in the 18th century and just keeps rolling along.

PITTSFIELD KEEPS EVOLVING...THE LEGEND CONTINUES

Make your own discoveries...Keep the legend going.

1735 - 1798

1735
- Boston land grant establishes township of Poontoosuck

1737
- Jacob Wendell buys Poontoosuck lots from Boston
- Establishes a partnership with John Stoddard

1750
- Indian attacks stop everything

1752
- First settler, Solomon Deming, moves to Poontoosuck

1753
- Charles Goodrich and others follow
- Settlers start discussion of Meeting House
- Indians attack again

1760
- First Meeting House raised
- Name change in the works

1761
- Poontoosuck changed to Pittsfield in honor of William Pitt, British Prime Minister
- Pittsfield incorporated as a town
- First service held in meeting house
- Parade of ministers begins
- First tavern opens on Arrowhead site

1765
- The Rev. Mr. Thomas Allen ordained as first minister of Congregational Church

1774
- First company of Minutemen in Pittsfield, formed under Captain David Noble

1777
- Rev. Mr. Thomas Allen leads troops in Battle of Bennington as "The Fighting Parson"

1779
- Pittsfield Bill of Rights written

1783
- Slavery officially ends in Pittsfield
- Festivities celebrating the signing of the Treaty of Paris and official end of Revolutionary War, held at John Chandler Williams house. Later known as the "Peace Party House"
- First Fourth of July Parade
- Hancock Village established by Shakers

1785
- Henry Van Schaack, a Tory from New York, builds a legendary Dutch Colonial Mansion

1786
- Ingersoll Tavern on North and Depot Streets, holds prisoners from Shay's Rebellion
- John Chandler Williams marries Lucretia Willliams, daughter of the Tory, Colonel Israel Williams

1790
- John Persip, a black stowaway from Portugal, comes to Pittsfield. Starts landscaping business, and a family which is still in town.

1791
- Site for New Meeting House selected, but a beautiful old elm tree is in the way
- Lucretia Williams saves the Pittsfield Elm from the ax
- Husband John Williams offers his property for meeting house
- Baseball by-law passed

1792
- Council permits Dr. Timothy Childs to open medicine store on Park Square and approves town burial ground on land near Meeting House
- Pittsfield Post Office opens
- George Washington appoints Post Master

1796
- Social libraries established
- Goodrich Tavern opens, one of Pittsfield's first "resorts"

1798
- The American Hotel opens on Park Square, Captain John Dickenson, Proprietor

1800 - 1859

1800
- Phinehas Allen moves to Pittsfield and starts The Pittsfield Sun
- Arthur Scholfield comes to Pittsfield with his wool carding machine
- James Colt builds legendary house
- The American Hotel changes name to William Clark Hotel. The Landlord, Captain Joseph Merrick, is a staunch Republican, who refuses to serve Federalists

1801
- Zenas Crane builds a paper mill on the Housatonic

1806
- Miss Nancy Hinsdale school opens. Later becomes Miss Hall's School

1807
- Elkanah Watson starts Berkshire Agricultural Society

1808
- Rev. Mr. Allen sells his original lots to Federalists, who open Pittsfield House on Park Square

1810
- Berkshire Bank, Pittsfield's first bank, opens on Park Square
- Elkanah Watson organizes the First Agricultural Fair in U.S. on Park Square

1812
- Lemuel Pomeroy buys Scholfield's textile business and starts Pittsfield Woolen and Cotton factory
- Campbell's Coffee House opens on Bank Row. Sort of a "resort" for British officers. Today: Patrick's Pub

1815
- Edward Newton marries Sarah Williams. He continues family philanthropy of John and Lucretia Williams

1818
- Berkshire Agricultural Bank opens

1823
- Berkshire Medical Institution, first Med School in Western Massachusetts opens on Park Square

1825
- Pontoosuc Woolen Mill chartered
- Thaddeus Clapp hired as Superintendent

1826
- Rev. Chester Dewey opens European-style Gymnasium school for boys

1832
- A new Town Hall is built on North side of Park Square. Lemuel Pomeroy pays for it
- St. Stephen's church, the First Episcopal Church in Pittsfield, built by Edward Newton

1835
- Berkshire Mutual Fire Insurance Company organized
- Nathan Willis is President

1840
- Pittsfield population about 4,000
- Pittsfield Baseball Club opens

1846
- Berkshire County Savings Bank opens on Park Square
- Blacks form Second Congregational Church and dedicate Meeting House on Onota Street
- Exchange Hotel opens on site of James Colt house

1849
- Dr. Oliver Wendell Holmes builds Holmesdale on Canoe Meadows, Great-Grandson of Jacob Wendell

1850
- Population of Pittsfield about 7000
- Pittsfield Library Association formed with 800 books
- Herman Melville comes to live at Arrowhead until 1863. He writes Moby Dick here
- West's Block opens
- Pittsfield Cemetery dedicated

1851
- George Nixon Briggs, former Massachusetts Governor, starts Berkshire Life Insurance Company on Park Square
- Western Massachusetts Mutual Fire Insurance Company starts

1853
- Pittsfield Coal Gas Company starts and gas brightens the town
- First President is Thomas F. Plunkett

1857
- Moses England opens his first store on North Street

1859
- First Intercollegiate Baseball Game between Williams/Amherst, played at Pittsfield Baseball Club: Baseball and Chess/Muscle and Mind
- Amherst wins

1860 - 1898

1860
- Octagon House built

1861
- Thomas F. Plunkett named President of Berkshire Life. Starts dynasty in insurance lasting 50 years

1862
- H. Davis & Co., department store, opens on North Street
- Rev. Samuel Harrison leaves church to work with the Abolitionist, Frederick Douglass. Soon appointed Chaplain of 54th Massachusetts Regiment of Black troops

1863
- Berkshire Medical School closes
- Council votes to find new ground for town cemetery

1865
- American House opens on North Street and Columbus. First hotel away from Park Square
- Pittsfield Elm Tree cut down: 340 years old, 128-feet tall
- Civil War ends

1868
- Berkshire Life Insurance moves to new corporate headquarters on West and North Streets. Stays 90-years

1869
- Temple Anshe Amunim founded. Second oldest Reform Congregation in the U.S.

1870
- Legislature changes library name to Berkshire Athenaeum: now has 2400 books

1871
- Burbank House built on North Street

1872
- Academy of Music opens
- Rev. Samuel Harrison returns to Pittsfield and Second Congregational Church
- Pleasure Park opens, a sportsman's delight. Today Deming Park

1874
- House of Mercy Hospital opens

1875
- Nesbit family businesses start. Nesbit Grocery, 3 Brother's Coal Co., Nesbit Garage and the Keator Group, spanning 130 years. Family still in town. Still in business.

1876
- The Allen cousins build the Berkshire Athenaeum on the South side of Park Square

1879
- Crane & Co. wins Government bid to produce U.S. bank note paper

1880
- Terry Clock Company formed
- Wood Brothers opens and sells musical instruments on North Street for 103 years

1881
- The Coliseum skating rink opens on Maplewood Avenue
- Grand Central Block opens. Name changes to Central Block. Still on North Street

1885
- William Stanley lights up North Street for Christmas
- A.H. Rice opens manufacturing facility to produce silk thread

1887
- Charles E. Hibbard moves his law firm to Pittsfield

1889
- Charter issued to The Co-op Bank

1890
- Council revises Charter and Pittsfield becomes a city
- Charles E. Hibbard elected first Mayor
- Stanley Electrical Manufacturing Company starts on Renne Avenue
- Abraham Burbank bequeaths money to develop city parks
- Burbank Park opens on Onota Lake

1891
- Kelton Miller buys weekly newspaper and starts a dynasty in publishing
- First trolley line built from depot to Pontoosuc Lake

1892
- George Burbank builds Wahconah Stadium

1893
- City Savings Bank opens on North Street
- Congregation Knesset Israel Synagogue organized
- Howard & Morrow open farm supply store on North Street

1895
- Elementary Schools open on Pontoosuc, Fenn, Orchard and other streets around town
- Charles L. Hibbard joins Father's firm

1896
- Pittsfield Cricket and Social Club organizes
- First Pittsfield High School opens on The Common for 600 students

1897
- Wealthy golfers organize 9-hole golf course between Williams Street and Dawes Avenue
- St. Joseph's School opens, first Parochial School in the city

1898
- Samuel and Carter Bowerman open elegant Wendell Hotel to honor their Father. Today, the Crowne Plaza on same site.
- Miss Hall's School for Girls officially founded
- Burgner's Farm starts delivering fresh food from the farm

1900 - 2006

1900
- Golfers buy Broadhall Mansion from the Morewood family. Golf moves to South Street and the Country Club of Pittsfield is started.
- J.M. Holmes Secretarial School opens on North Street
- Cooper's Coal opens...Hot Stuff
- Reverend Samuel Harrison dies

1903
- The General Electric Corporation buys Stanley Electrical Manufacturing Company
- Zenas Crane Jr. opens Berkshire Museum of Art and Natural History
- The curtain goes up at the Colonial Theatre

1904
- The Berkshire Eagle moves to Flatiron Building

1909
- YMCA opens
- Miss Hall's School moves to Holmes Road

1912
- Union Square Theatre opens. Soon named The Music Hall

1914
- Electric lights strung on Park Square Christmas Tree
- Harry's market opens on Wahconah Street. Still at same location. Now there are two Harry's plus a package store in town. Nichols family still the owner

1916
- Elizabeth Sprague Coolidge holds chamber music groups in her home on West Street

1918
- Coolidge Chamber Groups expand to South Mountain Concerts. Still playing in their own Concert Hall

1924
- Lou Gehrig hits home run from Wahconah Park into Housatonic River

1925
- W.T. Grant opens on North Street. Stays 44-years
- O'Connell Oil starts. Still carrying on the tradition

1926
- Puritan Bar/Restaurant opens on North Street. Today: The Lantern. Still going strong

1931
- New Pittsfield High School opens on East Street. One of the largest schools in New England

1932
- GE Plastics comes to Pittsfield

1936
- Petricca Construction Co., starts. Today, a unique Pittsfield landmark business known around the world for pre-cast concrete bridge components

1937
- GE Credit Union organized

1938
- WBRK, Pittsfield's first radio station, starts broadcasting

1940
- Winnie Davis Crane founds the Pittsfield Community Music School. Now: The Berkshire Music School on Wendell Avenue

1946
- The Berkshire Eagle starts WBEC and Pittsfield has two radio stations

1958
- Berkshire Life Insurance moves to new Colonial Building on South Street

1960
- Last Shakers at Hancock Village

1964
- First Hallowe'en Parade on North Street
- Quality Printing moves to town

1969
- Taconic High School opens. Comprehensive curriculum for 1150 students.

1971
- WBRG AM/FM appears as "alternative" radio
- West Side Clock Shop starts ticking on North Street

1977
- WUPE/WHOOPEE takes over when WBRG is sold. An eclectic radio programmer goes on the air

1979
- Guido's opens and "fresh" takes on new meaning

1980
- Berkshire Alarms starts to protect Pittsfield

1981
- 10th Ethnic Fair. 12,000 attend

1983
- Persip Day celebrated
- Paul Rich Home Furnishings opens on North Street
- Steve Valenti Men's Clothing store opens too

1988
- England Brothers closes its doors

1995
- Greylock Credit Union receives Federal Charter. (Formerly General Electric Credit Union)

1996
- General Dynamics Advanced Information Systems opens offices on Plastics Avenue

1998
- England Brothers building demolished. Legacy Bank goes up

2002
- Storefront Artist Project launched

2004
- Sheeptacular takes over the city
- Lichtenstein Art Center opens on Renne Avenue
- Joseph Scelsi Intermodal Transportation Center opens. Honors former Mayor and Councilman

2005
- First Pittsfield Jazz Festival
- Barrington Stage buys Music Hall and moves to Pittsfield

2006
- The Gilded Age in Pittsfield exhibit opens at Arrowhead
- Art of the Game Baseball exhibit starts 2-yr show
- Interprint opens new facility
- Ethnic Fair in the works

10th Ethnic Fair, 1981
12,000 attend

Courtesy of Lew Mahony and The Berkshire Eagle

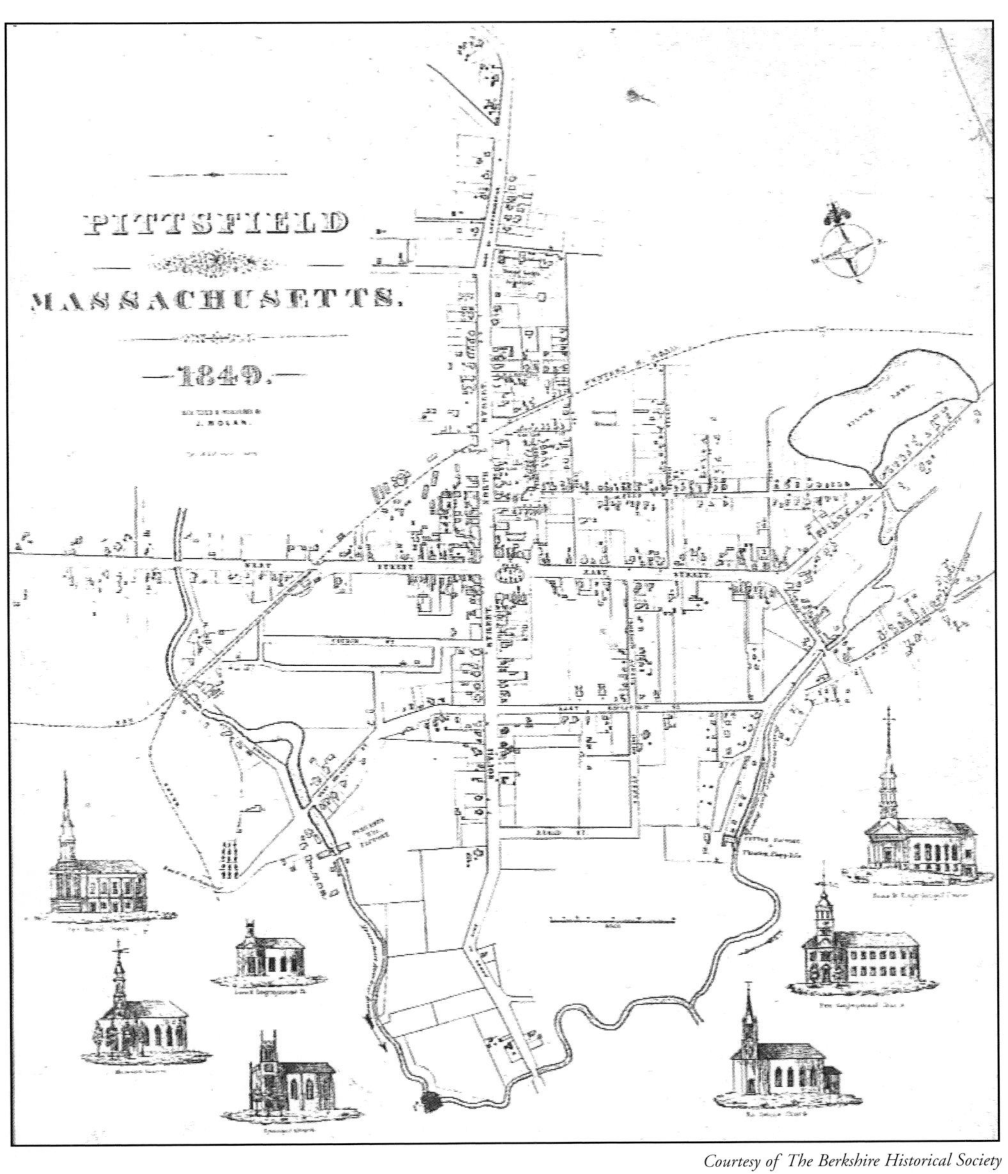

Courtesy of The Berkshire Historical Society

Always the center of action...Park Square

Park Square, c. 1770 *Courtesy of The Berkshire Historical Society*

Park Square, c. 1807 *Courtesy of The Berkshire Historical Society*

Park Square and the old elm tree, c. 1830 *Courtesy of The Berkshire Historical Society*

Park Square 1865: looking south at Bank Row *Courtesy of Berkshire Athenaeum*

By S. Barnes *Courtesy of Berkshire Athenaeum*

The Bulfinch Church and the Old Elm Tree

Lucretia's Elm Tree *Courtesy of The Berkshire Historical Society*

SITE OF THE
FIRST AGRICULTURAL FAIR
IN AMERICA
1810
AND
THE PITTSFIELD ELM
1524 - 1864

Photograph: Phyllis Kerle

The Plaque on Park Square

North Street, c. 1911 *Courtesy of Berkshire Athenaeum*

Courtesy of The Berkshire Historical Society

North Street, c. 1860

The tribute in Persip Park *Photograph: Phyllis Kerle*

Courtesy of The Berkshire Historical Society

North Street, 1850, the oldest photograph of the town

Courtesy of The Berkshire Historical Society

North Street, c. 1855

THANK YOU

many Pittsfield businesses, organizations,
individuals, acquaintances, and now friends.
THANKS for endless patience,
support and interest.

THANK YOU

Berkshire Athenaeum
Ann Marie Harris • Kathy Reilly
and colleagues in Local
History & Genealogy and
Reference Department

The Berkshire Historical Society
Pittsfield Cultural Council
Berkshire Visitors Bureau
Berkshire Chamber of Commerce
Cain Hibbard Myers & Cook pc
The Berkshire Eagle
WUPE
WBRK
WSI Intelligent Web Solutions
Pittsfield Trade & Commerce
Auxier Computers

Brenda Burdick
Wendy Webster Coakley
Mary Farley
Mike MacDonald
Larry Kratka
Ed Reilly
Arthur Stein
Conrad Bernier
Gerald Lee
Matthew Kerwood

J. Peter Bergman
David Bissaillon
Lynn Mason
Andrew H. Mick
Ellen Ruberto
Betty Rich
Tom Rich
Chuck Brush
Roger Brissette
Michael Sobon
Pam Knisley
Peter Hopkins
Giles Prett
Leh-Wen Yau
Dave Smart
Jayne Church
Pam Malumphy
Joe Toole
Steve Valenti
David Showalter

Kelton Burbank
Mark Miller
Eleanor Persip
Tom & Helen Plunkett
Andrew and Kelly Blau

SPECIAL APPRECIATION

Quality Printing Company, Inc
General Dynamics Advanced Information Systems
The Berkshire Gas Company
Berkshire Life Insurance Company of America
Pittsfield CO-OP Bank
Paul Rich & Sons Home Furnishings
David Ward

Robert & Kathryn Benedett Lupoli

William J. Bartz
June Roy-Martin
Rebecca Smith
Lewis H. Mahony
William R. Wilson, Jr.

Dedicated to

Margaret Rector

A legend in her own time
An unforgettable friend

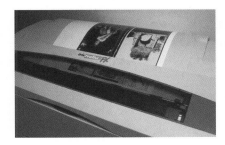

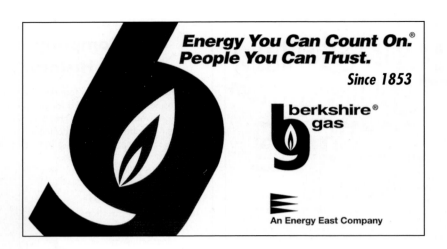

PRODUCTION TEAM

Printer: Quality Printing Co., Inc.
Researcher/Author: Phyllis E. Kerle
Historian/Editor: William J. Bartz
Local Advisor: Lewis H. Mahony
Finance Manager: William R. Wilson, BVB
Technical Advisor: Giles Prett
Book Designer: Mark Tomasi
Cover: Kristi Tirrell
Proofreader: Adelle Michaud
Scans: Ann Marie Harris, Berkshire Athenaeum
Tim Auxier, Auxier Computers

Pittsfield Keeps Evolving...

The Legend Continues